Penguin Critical Studies

Heart of Darkness

Richard Adams completed his undergraduate and graduate studies in English language and literature at St Catherine's College, Oxford, where he also taught for several years during the 1960s. Subsequently, as an English teacher at Lord Williams's School, Thame, he wrote several school and academic texts, including *Appropriate English*, *Into Shakespeare* and *Teaching Shakespeare*, and was invited to undertake the general editorship of two Longman series: Longman Study Texts and Practical Approaches to Literary Criticism. He has published editions of three Shakespeare plays for Macmillan, as well as editions of works by Conrad, Shaffer, Russell, Ayckbourn and (most recently) Iris Murdoch. Since 1986, Richard Adams has held the post of Professor of English at the California State University in Sacramento. He is also a director of the California Literature Project.

Penguin Critical Studies
Advisory Editor: Bryan Loughrey

Joseph Conrad

Heart of Darkness

Richard Adams

Penguin Books

PENGUIN BOOKS

Published by the Penguin Group
Penguin Books Ltd, 27 Wrights Lane, London W8 5TZ, England
Penguin Books USA Inc., 375 Hudson Street, New York, New York 10014, USA
Penguin Books Australia Ltd, Ringwood, Victoria, Australia
Penguin Books Canada Ltd, 10 Alcorn Avenue, Toronto, Ontario, Canada M4V 3B2
Penguin Books (NZ) Ltd, 182–190 Wairau Road, Auckland 10, New Zealand

Penguin Books Ltd, Registered Offices: Harmondsworth, Middlesex, England

First published 1991
10 9 8 7 6 5 4 3

Printed in England by Clays Ltd, St Ives plc
Filmset in 9/11 pt Monophoto Times

What is truth? said jesting Pilate;
and would not stay for an answer.

FRANCIS BACON

Contents

Part Three

Postscript

Note

Page references in the text refer to the Penguin edition of
Heart of Darkness.

1. Introduction

Many works of fiction, particularly those written before the end of the nineteenth century, provide us with some notion of their subject-matter or focus before we actually embark on a reading of the text. They do so by means of their title-pages. One, for instance, purports to be an account of the travels of a man named Gulliver, while another proclaims itself to be the autobiographical narrative of a clergyman from the town of Wakefield. With a third, we are led to expect a study of the kind of provincial life carried on in a place called Middlemarch. Other titles reveal in advance the identity of a pivotal character or characters – from Pamela and Joseph Andrews and Jane Eyre to Emma and Dombey (and his son) and Tess and Jude. The names themselves may not tell us much about what to expect in terms either of personality or of career, but at least they give us some idea of whom we should be watching. Similarly, with *North and South* or *The Mill on the Floss* or *A Tale of Two Cities* we are prepared for some kind of geographical focus, whether fictitious or real. Still other titles – such as Jane Austen's *Persuasion*, *Pride and Prejudice* and *Sense and Sensibility* – indicate key ideas or themes or ruling passions.

With *Heart of Darkness*, first published in the spring of 1899, the case is rather different. The phrase is ambiguous, deeply suggestive and logically problematical. At first sight, it is difficult to envisage what kind of signpost to the text it can possibly be.

The ambiguity derives from our natural uncertainty over the force of the word 'of': does it signify composition or location? Are we about to learn about a heart made of darkness – a heart that *is* somehow dark – or a place which lies at the very centre of an area of darkness? That Conrad intended this ambiguity is suggested by the fact that, though he consistently referred to the piece during its composition as *The Heart of Darkness*, a title which tends to favour the 'location' signification, he dropped the definite article on publication.

Then there is the matter of the range of commonly accepted meanings and associations of 'heart' and 'darkness', and the fact that the two words stand, in many respects, at opposite poles. 'Heart' has a powerful positive force: from its primary denotation of the physical organ on which all animal life depends, it comes to be representative of the life-force itself, as well as of life-enhancing qualities and emotions such as goodness, compassion, courage, love. 'Darkness', on the other hand, has distinctly negative overtones. In a whole host of world mythologies, it is associated with chaos and disorder, the condition to combat which light and life were created. The term 'the Dark Ages' was coined to identify a period of relative unenlightenment in the cultural and intellectual life of early medieval Europe. Because human beings do not naturally function well in the dark, it came to be thought of as the home and haven of all those things – intangible as well as tangible – of which people were unsure or fearful or suspicious. It suggested the unknown, the unknowable, the unintelligible, the ignorant, the sinister, the secret. The English language still abounds in expressions which reflect these associations: a friend asks me what I have been doing lately and, in telling him, I extract a promise that he will 'keep it dark'. In ensuring that other members of our circle are kept ignorant of my activities in this way, I am deliberately leaving them 'in the dark'. But because these other people are aware that I am up to something, without knowing exactly what that something is, they begin to think of me as a 'dark horse' and to speak of my activities – perhaps ironically, perhaps not – as 'dark deeds'.

From such negative attributions, it is but a short step to the fundamental association of darkness with evil. For pre-electric man, darkness was the impenetrable cloak under which crimes and diabolical acts of all kinds were committed: not for nothing was Satan known as 'the Prince of Darkness'. In medieval and Renaissance art, he was indeed commonly portrayed as being black-faced, as were the hapless souls that fell into his grasp. Shakespeare's Macbeth greets the servant who brings him news of the arrival of the English force that is to topple him from power with the curse 'the devil damn thee black'.

It was a perverse and unhealthy logic that extended these associations of ignorance and evil to the negro – the 'darky', as he was called in popular slang – the aboriginal inhabitant of Africa, the 'dark' continent. The conversion of pagan tribes to Christianity and their political and social 'improvement' were figuratively expressed as the bringing of light into a dark wilderness, the benign imposition on chaos of a productive order.

The title *Heart of Darkness* is, then, crammed with complex and shifting associations. For Ian Watt, it consists of more than the mere yoking together of two stock metaphors as a means of designating, on the one hand, the centre of benighted Africa, and on the other, a quintessentially evil person (one whose heart is literally made of darkness).[1] He draws attention to the logical implausibility of attributing to

2

the more concrete of the two terms, 'heart', a strategic centrality within a formless and infinite abstraction. 'How', he asks, 'can something inorganic like darkness have an organic centre of life and feeling? How can a shapeless absence of light compact itself into a shaped and pulsing presence?' The problem Watt identifies here is compounded, moreover, by the moral paradox of a 'good' entity (the heart) exercising control over an 'evil' one (darkness).

In sum, as we turn to the text for the first time, we need to be aware that the title *Heart of Darkness* does not work at all in the way that *Nicholas Nickleby* and *Crotchet Castle* or – among Conrad's own writings – *Typhoon* and *The Nigger of the Narcissus* work. If we deduce from it anything about the narrative we are about to encounter, perhaps it should be that that narrative may also have its ambiguities, its suggestiveness and its problems of logic.

Part One

2. The *Nellie* and Her Crew (*pages 27–8*)

Any reader of Conrad who comes to *Heart of Darkness* reared exclusively on a diet of the author's sea-stories might be excused, after glancing at the opening paragraphs, for thinking that he or she was about to be served up with more of the same. The *Nellie*, for all that she is temporarily becalmed on the Thames near Gravesend, is bound downriver towards the sea, where any number of adventures may be awaiting her. And, as if to reinforce the impression that this is indeed to be a tale of the sea and ships, the text is liberally seasoned with the sort of technical jargon likely to pack the average reader smartly off to a glossary of nautical terms for assistance. We are told that 'the *Nellie*, a cruising yawl, swung to her anchor' and that 'the flood had made' so that 'the only thing for it was to come to'. There is mention of 'the offing', of 'peaked' sails and 'varnished sprits'.

With the third paragraph, however, there comes a shift of emphasis. We learn that, for all his nautical and reassuringly pilot-like appearance, the boat's captain is not a professional sailor but a company director. Or rather, the other way about: 'The Director of Companies was our captain and our host.' The picture begins to focus more clearly: the narrator's companions are weekend sailors, men engaged in city business of one kind or another, invited by the *Nellie*'s owner to join him for a social cruise down the Thames.

The entire group consists of five men, identified for us as the Director, the Lawyer, the Accountant, Marlow (the only one of them referred to by name and the only one, as we are later told, who is still a professional seaman) and the narrator. The bond between them is the fact that they have all at some time in their lives 'followed the sea'. The narrator refers to this fact at the beginning of the fourth paragraph, where he also touches, in passing, on his having said as much 'somewhere' else. This somewhere is at the beginning of Conrad's narrative 'Youth', where the identical company is to be found 'sitting around a mahogany table that reflected the bottle, the claret-glasses, and our faces as we leaned on our elbows' and it is made clear that all five of its members had started life in the merchant service. None of the men is described in any great detail in the opening pages of *Heart of Darkness*; however, in referring briefly to the appearance or actions of each, the narrator flashes across the reader's consciousness a number of ideas and images that are developed later in the story.

With the first mention of the Director, for instance, we are reminded of the deceptiveness of appearances. As he stands in the bows of his boat and gazes seaward he arouses in his companions feelings of affection and deep trust. The narrator remarks that he looks like a pilot, 'which to a seaman is trustworthiness personified', and suggests that he ought to be working 'out there in the luminous estuary'. But he is not: his employment lies behind him, in the city of London, 'within the brooding gloom'. The suggestion is that any kind of appearance, whether good or bad, is not to be taken on face value.

The Lawyer and Accountant are treated to rather briefer descriptions. The former, who seems to be the senior member of the party, is stretched out on the deck, enjoying the benefit – on account 'of his many years and many virtues' – of the only cushion and the only rug available. The latter has brought out a box of dominoes and is halfheartedly building little structures ('toying architecturally') with the pieces. The narrator's use of the word 'bones' reminds us that, prior to mass-production, dominoes were often made of ebony inlaid with bone or ivory, and that bone and ivory were for centuries mistakenly believed to be the same substance.

Last to be mentioned is Marlow, whose sitting position is described by the narrator with great precision:

Marlow sat cross-legged right aft, leaning against the mizzen-mast. He had sunken cheeks, a yellow complexion, a straight back, an ascetic aspect, and, with his arms dropped, the palms of hands outwards, resembled an idol. (page 28)

As William Bysshe Stein has pointed out, Marlow is here sitting in the so-called lotus posture, familiar to us from its representation in the Buddhist art of India and the Orient.[1] This posture is the one adopted as a prerequisite to Yoga meditation, contemplation and absorption, and it suggests that Marlow 'is ready to engage in an exercise of intense introspection', with the expectation that it will lead to some kind of personal enlightenment. That we are intended to register this connection is made clear by the fact that the narrator goes on to refer to Marlow's Buddha-like bearing on three further occasions in the course of *Heart of Darkness*.

The untrustworthiness of appearances ... the idea that people and things may not always be what they seem; a man lying full-length on the deck of a boat; another halfheartedly building little structures with domino pieces ... bone and ivory ... something white inlaid, grafted, imposed on something black; a third man composing himself for meditation, self-examination, in the hope of enlightenment: such are the ideas and images that we glimpse at the opening of *Heart of Darkness*, ideas and images whose significance becomes clearer as the story progresses.

The narrator adds nothing about himself to this thumbnail gallery of the *Nellie*'s passengers. However, his observations in the opening pages of the story – for all that he implies that a number of them reflect the corporate consciousness of the group – reveal a sensitive and essentially optimistic being.[2] It is he, for example, who articulates the importance of the sea-bond to him and his companions: 'Besides holding our hearts together through long periods of separation, it had the effect of making us tolerant of each other's yarns – and even convictions.' Their estrangement from the sea has introduced diversity of interest, opinion and attitude among the members of the group. The beliefs that any one of them holds and expresses will not necessarily find sympathy or understanding on the part of the others, though the comradeship born of their shared past experiences ought to be enough to ensure a respectful hearing. Each reserves the right to put his personal construction on the tale that another tells; each makes his own decision about accepting or rejecting the philosophical base on which that tale is reared.

As readers, as eavesdroppers on the narrative of *Heart of Darkness*, we are invited to do the same.

3. The Setting (*pages 27–9*)

The *Nellie*, then, is in a kind of limbo, waiting with her five passengers for the turn of the tide in order to slip down the Thames estuary towards the open sea. As she swings to her anchor, off the ominously-named port of Gravesend, the narrator, from his position on deck, is able to observe the play of light and shadow as the sun begins to set over the river.

The effect is, in fact, a somewhat unexpected one. The Thames, in its journey towards the sea, flows roughly from west to east – that is, away from the setting sun – though it takes a northward turn for a few miles below Gravesend. As he looks seaward, the narrator notes the luminous quality of the light over the water (in the offing), that, indeed, sea and sky seem 'welded together without a joint'. Only along the twin flat shorelines, running out to sea, is there a little haze, which he describes as having a fairy delicacy: 'gauzy . . . radiant', hanging 'in diaphanous folds'. When, however, he looks upstream, towards the west where the remaining light of day should be stronger, he observes the air above Gravesend to be dark, and that, further back still, this darkness is intensified, seemingly 'condensed into a mournful gloom, brooding motionless' over the city of London, 'the biggest, and the greatest, town on earth'. That there is something sinister about this darkness is suggested not only by its location and by the narrator's choice of words to describe it, but also by the fact that – as we have already observed – it surprises him that such a loved and trusted companion as the *Nellie*'s captain should pursue a career not in the estuary, with its radiant light, but 'within the brooding gloom'. The darkness becomes 'more sombre' every minute, and, when at last the sun sinks below the western horizon, it is almost as if it has been 'stricken to death by the touch of that gloom brooding over a crowd of men'. The inference, however, is not that London and everything that goes on within its confines are somehow contaminated by the hovering darkness, rather that the darkness is an image or physical embodiment of all that the 'monstrous town' (that is, one devoid of humanity) stands for. Indeed, once night has fallen, the gloom is replaced by 'a lurid glare' that marks the position of the city 'ominously on the sky'. We are not told precisely what makes London monstrous in the narrator's view, though we know that it is a place where companies flourish, where anonymous directors, lawyers and accountants make their living.

10

Nor does the Thames seem quite its old, familiar self as the narrator gazes about him. There is something mysterious about it, reaching into the unknown distance 'like the beginning of an interminable waterway', one that goes on for ever and whose ultimate destination is uncertain. Though, in this moment of utter serenity, the 'venerable stream' appears 'unruffled' almost to the point of motionlessness, in fact it flows inexorably, not merely to the immediately waiting sea, but beyond it 'to the uttermost ends of the earth'.

The ambivalence which characterizes the narrator's description of the surroundings in which he and his companions find themselves is to be further detected in his record of their conversation evoking 'the great spirit of the past', the 'memories of men and ships' borne 'to the rest of home or to the battles of the sea' upon the waters of the Thames. They envisage a pageant of the nation's heroes, those who have deserved its gratitude and pride through their service as adventurers, settlers, fighters, merchants, 'hunters for gold . . . pursuers of fame'.

Sir Francis Drake and Sir John Franklin are given special mention among the 'great knights-errant of the sea'. At first glance these seem, indeed, names to conjure with, synonymous with the heroic quest and the heroic ordeal. Closer inspection, however, reveals other associations, of uncontrolled expansionism and tragic miscalculation. For all his accidental achievement in circumnavigating the globe, Drake was, for much of his career, little more than a licensed pirate, bent on plundering and destroying where he could. The ironic image of his flagship, the *Golden Hind*, as a pregnant animal about to give birth to a fortune – 'her round flanks full of treasure' – reminds us that the highly productive exploits of her sea-captains did much, in the popular imagination, to compensate for the Virgin Queen's own problematical infertility, even though she herself might have wished it otherwise. Although Franklin lived in a less colourful age than Drake, his ill-fated expedition to find a north-west passage round the top of Canada to the Pacific during the 1840s was similarly inspired by material interests. Scientific exploration is seldom an end in itself, but commonly acts as a precursor to colonial or commercial enterprise. In the event, both of Franklin's ships, the *Erebus* and *Terror* – whose very names, taken together, signify the horrors of hell[1] – were lost in the Arctic ice along with all but a handful of their officers and men. The catalogue of such endeavours may, indeed, in the narrator's words, be a 'gigantic tale', but it is a tale with many a bitter twist. He acknowledges – and here it is impossible to separate his viewpoint from those of his companions – that 'the dreams of men, the seed of commonwealths, the germs of empires' have in the past depended for their realization and growth as much on the sword of enforcement as on the torch of enlightenment. The 'sacred fire' whose spark was carried into the darkness, 'the mystery of an unknown earth', was paradoxically kindled in the very place over which the brooding gloom now hangs.

As if to underscore the point, as dusk advances it brings with it a spate of activity. In the 'luminous space' of day, all had seemed motionless: the *Nellie*'s sails had not so much as fluttered and those of the barges had 'seemed to stand still'. Now, however, the lights of ships move in the fairway – 'a great stir of lights going up and down' – as if to emphasize the association between mercantile venture and the cover of dark. A little later in the narrative, the traffic of the city is expressed in the image of different coloured flames 'pursuing, overtaking, joining, crossing each other – then separating slowly or hastily' on the surface of the unsleeping river.

4. Marlow's Preamble (*pages 29–32*)

'And this also ... has been one of the dark places of the earth.' Marlow's words sound a variation of the continuing theme: before it became a centre of commercial enterprise from which men might carry the lamp of civilization into the 'unknown earth', London was itself a mysterious and benighted place. Nor is that time, in terms of the earth's history, so very long past. Nineteen hundred years ago seems like 'the other day' and the darkness, he asserts, 'was here yesterday'. The light of civilization is little more than a flash of lightning in the night of time, and darkness the norm that it but briefly interrupts. Marlow imagines what the place must have seemed like to the Romans when they arrived, first as soldier-adventurers sailing up the Thames, later as settlers living on its banks. In doing so, he touches on conditions and hardships typically experienced by explorers in every period of history – from the British 'knights-errant' on whose achievements he and his sailing companions have just been reflecting to the central characters of the story he is about to relate.

To the trireme commander used to plying the friendly Mediterranean but 'suddenly ordered north', for instance, Britain would have seemed like 'the very end of the world', with its leaden seas and smoky skies. There would have been sandbanks to negotiate along the course of the river itself, and marshes, forests and savages to deter him from venturing ashore too often – the only relief from the pervasive hostility of the environment being found at one or other of the military outposts 'lost in a wilderness'. Then there would have been the inclemency of the climate, the perils of disease and everywhere – 'in the air, in the water, in the bush' – the presence of death. All of which Marlow characterizes as 'the darkness'. He goes on to suggest how such a man might manage to survive: perhaps by closing his mind to the difficulties of the situation – by shutting out the darkness, as it were – and just getting on with the job in hand, perhaps by fixing his sights on the day when this particular tour of duty would be over and he could move on to something more congenial.

Primitive Britain would have been no less unappealing to and fraught with dangers for the second type of pioneer that Marlow envisages – the 'decent young citizen in a toga', the civilian who, on account of some financial imprudence at home, found himself obliged to 'mend his

13

fortunes' in the colonies. The very marshes and woods from whose menace the ship-commander could retreat to the safety of his vessel, this man would have had to confront and endure at first hand. His home would have become one of those lost outposts, linked to the outside world by the occasional visit of a supply-ship, and there he would have been exposed to the psychological pressures of living in an alien terrain, feeling 'the savagery, the utter savagery' shutting on him like a trap. Marlow dwells feelingly on the predicament of the young settler, surrounded by a people whose strange, savage ways he would have entirely failed to understand and would, inevitably, have come to hate. For him, unlike the commander, there would have been no escape, only a reluctant but growing fascination with the incomprehensible world around him and a preoccupation with 'growing regrets, the longing to escape, the powerless disgust, the surrender, the hate' as he is overtaken by the moral darkness that has entered his soul.

Must it always be so? Must civilized values inevitably be subject to atavistic regression, a return to primitive beliefs and mores? Must the light of human achievement always be smothered by the darkness? Marlow - perhaps half apologetically, sensing some animosity on the part of his audience – draws a distinction between Roman imperialism and modern colonialism. The former, he argues, was based on nothing more than the accident of strength, on the principle of grabbing what can be got for the sheer sake of grabbing. 'It was just robbery with violence, aggravated murder on a great scale, and men going at it blind.' This is what led to its corruption from within and eventual demise. What saves modern (and, presumably, British) colonialism, by way of contrast, is its possession of an ideal, a philosophy, a rationale for action: 'an idea at the back of it; not a sentimental pretence but an idea.' And what saves the present-day pioneer from going the way of his Roman counterpart is the fact that this ideal provides him with something to believe in, something in which he can place his faith. The ideal that Marlow has in mind, though he does not present his argument very clearly at this point, would appear to be that of 'efficiency'. Ian Watt has suggested that he uses the word as signifying a belief in the moral worth of labour – a sense popularized by nineteenth-century Social Darwinians. Thus, 'the work-ethic of the British colonist fortifies him against the darkness, while the Roman, lacking this devotion, was more vulnerable.'[1]

5. Marlow's Narrative Method (*pages 30–32*)

Before recounting Marlow's impressions of early Roman Britain, the narrator comments on his friend's characteristic method of telling a story. He compares Marlow's yarns with those told by other seamen, which – he asserts – 'have a direct simplicity, the whole meaning of which lies within the shell of a cracked nut'. The implication here seems to be that the significance of the conventional sea-tale is both limited and unambiguous; we get at it by prying open the cracked shell of the narrative. Marlow, on the other hand, found the meaning of an episode 'not inside like a kernel but outside'. For him, the narrative was the nut itself, enclosed within the shell of its own meaning, a meaning which the primary narrator further likens to the haze that surrounds a glow of light, 'one of these misty halos that sometimes are made visible by the spectral illumination of moonshine'. The significance, in this case, is neither limited nor unambiguous. Its various layers, like lunar-rings, vary in intensity and clarity and reach out into infinity. And they may only be apparent when the narrative is focused in a certain way, only perceived when viewed from a particular angle.

Marlow himself sanctions this interpretation of his narrative method in the apologia with which he prefaces his story. The effect of his experiences upon him (the real point of his tale), he maintains, can be fully understood only when they are presented against their proper background, in the context, that is, of his movements, observations and encounters. The only reason he feels justified in bothering his listeners much with details of his adventures is that they seem 'somehow to throw a kind of light on everything about me – and into my thoughts'. He recalls the sombreness, the pitifulness of what happened, but adds the remark that it was in no way out of the ordinary, as if such occurrences are to be regarded as life's norms. His final remark on the subject is strongly reminiscent of the narrator's 'misty halo' image: though they had an illuminating effect both on the physical world around him and on his own mental world, his experiences at the time impressed him as being 'not very clear'.

That the primary narrator himself finds it difficult to come to terms with – and, indeed, does not fully understand the workings of – such a narrative approach is revealed in his comment, as their companion warms to his theme, about the audience's being fated to listen to one of

Marlow's 'inconclusive experiences'. It is also reflected in his paren-
thetical judgement that Marlow's natural inclination to keep himself
out of his story as much as possible is a weakness, in that it betrays a
lack of sympathy with his audience's interests. This remark comes as a
timely reminder to the reader that *Heart of Darkness* is a work which
should be approached and evaluated on its own terms. We are unlikely
to get much out of Marlow's narrative unless we can recognize that its
various meanings may only be glimpsed fitfully, in the course of our
journey through the tale, but that, at such moments, they will very likely
out-range our imaginings.

6. Background to Adventure (*pages 32–5*)

The following two or three pages of the text are devoted to Marlow's establishing the background to his adventure. In the course of his doing so, he makes several references which help reinforce – and, in some cases, develop – the story's central ideas and images, a principal one of which is the idea of reversal, of things coming out contrary to our expectations, of things being not quite what they at first seemed.

He begins, for example, by recalling an occasion when, after 'a lot of Indian Ocean, Pacific, China Seas', he spent some time on shore leave in London. He jokingly refers to his persistent invasion of his friends' offices and homes as having its origins in some 'heavenly mission to civilize' them. His choice of words is, of course, plainly ironic, turning on its head as it does the commonly accepted notion that the city – and London of all cities – is a cradle of civilization; that those, furthermore, who spend long years at sea are, by virtue of their calling and circumstances, themselves largely cut off from its benefits. There is an implicit link between Marlow's irony and the image which earlier in *Heart of Darkness* depicted London as a 'monstrous town', customarily mantled with a brooding gloom. As if to establish beyond question the flavour of the paragraph from which it comes, this particular remark is followed in rapid succession by a string of paradoxes: that it is possible to get tired of resting, that seeking work is 'the hardest work on earth' and that a seaman may look for a ship but the ships will not necessarily look at him.

These transpositions and contradictions, trivial as they are, prepare us for one that is considerably more sustained and closer to the central concerns of the story. Marlow explains how, since boyhood, he has been fascinated with the idea of exploring some of the uncharted regions, the 'blank spaces', of the globe, and how his obsession has always been greatest with one place in particular, 'the biggest, the most blank'. He relates how, during the stay in London previously referred to, his attention was drawn to a map of this country displayed in a Fleet Street window. By this time, the blank spaces remembered from his boyhood had largely been filled 'with rivers and lakes and names'. The region in question 'had ceased to be a blank space of delightful mystery – a white patch for a boy to dream gloriously over. It had become a place of darkness' (page 33).

17

should have
become illuminated

The principal equations established so far in the story have been those of darkness with mystery and lightness with a purging of that mystery. Marlow's perception, however, continues to question such equations and serves to reinforce the notion that civilization creates its own darkness, has its own grim secrets.

As he examines the map in the window, Marlow's interest is aroused in particular by the river which curls like a huge snake over the vast territory. It does not take him long to remember that there is 'a big concern', a suitably anonymous 'Company', trading along that river, and to decide to apply for command of one of the steamboats that it employs for the purpose. His choosing in this way to exchange a life at sea for the direct furtherance of commercial interests shows Marlow reversing the process by which his companions aboard the *Nellie*, in their casual jaunt down the Thames, seek relief from the stresses of life within the 'brooding gloom' of the city.

He expresses his absorption with the idea of working on this 'mighty big river' in a remarkable metaphor: in his imagination, the river becomes the snake which it resembles and, in that guise, exercises an irresistible fascination over him, just as it might a bird – 'a silly little bird' – on which it is about to prey. Like some defenceless but foolish creature, Marlow is about to be swallowed up by a much greater force over which he has absolutely no control. As if to emphasize this notion, in a small but significant image-shift, he accords to the snake possession of the sort of power over man that man is more usually reckoned to have over snakes: it is able to charm him. In this way we see the river unnaturally exercising its sinister, even fatal, attraction and are reminded of the powerless fascination felt by the young Roman settler beside an alien Thames.

Marlow's imaginative reconstruction (a couple of pages earlier) of the frustrations, dangers and psychological disorientation experienced by the Roman colonizers of primitive Britain is, of course, the work of a mature vision. His use at this point of the expression 'all the glories of exploration' is ironical, to be read aright as part of his boyish passion for maps and projected travels to exotic places. Certainly, his badgering of his continental relatives to exert their influence in securing him command of one of the Company's steamboats is the result of his simple interest in work – or, to put it more bluntly, his desperation for a job – rather than of any glamorous or high-minded notions.

The ominous circumstances under which a position is eventually offered him do nothing to undermine Marlow's enthusiasm – rather the contrary:

It appears the Company had received news that one of their captains had been killed in a scuffle with the natives. This was my chance, and it made me the more anxious to go. (page 34)

Marlow's account of the death of Fresleven, the man whose shoes he has been appointed to fill, contains further examples both of contradictory appearances and of bitter irony. Fresleven, he tells us, had a reputation among his fellows for being 'the gentlest, quietest creature that ever walked on two legs'. Yet it does not surprise Marlow to learn that this same man should have hammered a village chief with a stick on account of 'a misunderstanding about some hens'. The inconsistency is simply explained: 'he had been a couple of years already out there engaged in the noble cause.' The conditions under which men exist in order to bring some light into the pervasive darkness take a heavy toll, can have unforeseen and horrifying consequences. By the time Marlow comes upon his predecessor's remains, 'the grass growing through his ribs was tall enough to hide his bones' – a reminder of the narrator's earlier picture of the Accountant on board the *Nellie* toying with the dominoes. The Company had apparently made no effort to retrieve and bury Fresleven, just as the steamer he had commanded had abandoned him to his fate, leaving the settlement where the murder took place 'in a bad panic'. The villagers – fearing a retribution which, in the event, never materialized – had also fled the scene, so that now their 'huts gaped black, rotting, all askew within the fallen enclosures'. At the end of his account of the episode, Marlow asks whimsically after the fate of the hens – two more silly little birds casually consumed, like Fresleven, in the maw of larger issues. His sardonic attitude to the entire business is conveyed in Marlow's description of it as 'glorious' – a word which has already, in the space of only a few pages, shifted its meaning radically.

7. The Company Headquarters (*pages 35–9*)

This episode, with its intricate web of images and allusions, has been the subject of extensive critical analysis and commentary. Some scholars[1] see striking similarities between Marlow's journey in *Heart of Darkness* and the journeys described in Virgil's *Aeneid* (Book Six) and Dante's *Inferno*, suggesting that an acknowledgement of its conscious use of epic machinery is a necessary prelude to our proper understanding of Conrad's novella. For them, the characters and actions described in these few pages are extremely precise in their import, and seem to lend themselves to a suitably limited symbolic interpretation of the text. Critics like Watt,[2] on the other hand – picking up on the various clues that the author provides as to how Marlow's narrative is to be read – prefer not to confine the episode's wide-ranging associations within too narrow a frame of reference.

The Company's headquarters is located not in London but on the continent, in a city of which Marlow declares that it 'always makes [him] think of a whited sepulchre'. That the Company could as well, however, be operating from the British capital as from this particular nameless city is suggested by the fact that the story is being told aboard a boat moored off a place called Gravesend. 'Whited sepulchre' is a term used by Christ in St Matthew's Gospel (23:27) to typify those who are not what they seem: hypocrites who disguise their moral corruption with shows of virtue, who are 'like ... whited sepulchres, which indeed appear beautiful outward, but are within full of dead men's bones, and of all uncleanness'. Marlow makes clear its application to the city, and, by extension, to the Company whose activities dominate the conversation of its inhabitants, by his repeated references – both open and veiled – to death. There is 'dead silence' in the street in which the Company's offices are located, the place to which he is about to be dispatched is 'dead in the centre' of the map that hangs on the waiting-room wall, its river being likened a second time to a fascinating and 'deadly' snake, while the entire building seems as unnaturally silent as 'a house in a city of the dead'. Then there is his reference to the grass sprouting between the stones of the street, directly reminiscent of the grass growing through the dead Fresleven's ribs, mentioned only a few lines earlier. And, as if Marlow fully expects to follow his predecessor in this as in all other things, he ironically hails the women who keep the

20

outer room with the defiant greeting traditionally spoken by gladiators selected to fight in the arenas of ancient Rome: *'Ave! ... Morituri te salutant'* ('Hail ... those who are about to die salute you').

The anonymity of these two women is consonant with their surroundings. Beyond the fact that the one is young and slim while the other is old and fat, we are told precious little about their appearance. Their functions within the office are equally briefly sketched, the former being responsible for ushering and introducing visitors, the latter seemingly spending her entire existence 'scrutinizing their cheery and foolish faces with unconcerned old eyes'. The detail about them that strikes both Marlow and the reader most forcibly is their knitting. Who are they? What do they stand for? What does their knitting signify? Analogies have been drawn, variously, with the Fates of classical mythology (the three goddesses who shape, weave and finally cut the threads of human destiny),[3] the Cumaean Sibyl, the vengeful *tricoteuses* who sat knitting at the foot of the guillotine during the French Revolution, the figures of Sin and Death who guard the gates of Hell in Milton's *Paradise Lost*, and – not surprisingly – the blood-hungry crowds that attended gladiatorial combats in ancient Rome.

Wherever our individual sympathies may lie in such matters, we should not overlook those areas in which Marlow's guidance is quite explicit. In the first place, the women are knitting 'black wool as for a warm pall', a detail which not only ties in with the prevailing imagery of darkness and death but also serves as a metaphor for the colonial expansion in which the Company is engaged. The process of knitting entails the manipulation of a raw material in order to create some new and serviceable artefact, while the fine, densely curling nature of negro hair has sometimes led to those who possess it being referred to as 'woolly-heads'. (Indeed, Conrad has Marlow himself employ the term later in *Heart of Darkness*.) The knitting of black wool thus suggests the calculated exploitation of the negro and his environment by the Company and its white servants. We note, further, that the knitting is carried on seemingly without thought or pause – even when more important duties or courtesies beckon – and that it is pursued with feverish haste. Secondly, Marlow is very precise about the effect that these women have on him. He is troubled by the 'swift and indifferent placidity', the 'unconcerned wisdom' of the look darted at him by the older of the two when he emerges from his cursory interview with the 'great man'. Like the witches in Shakespeare's *Macbeth* (and we note the cat on her lap and the wart on her cheek), she seems 'uncanny and fateful' – appears, that is to say, to be possessed of supernatural insight into the future.

21

Moreover, she and her companion guard 'the door of Darkness'. They guard literally, of course, in their role as concierges of the Company's offices, but Marlow's phrase also suggests their metaphorical relationship with the Company's activities in general, and the place to which its hapless employees are sent in particular. We are also, perhaps, reminded of the funerary statues found in ancient tombs and – especially in the figure of the younger woman who 'pilots' the visitors from one room to another – of the mythical boatman Charon whose function it was, upon their entrance to Hades, to ferry dead souls across the River Styx.

The mechanical impassivity of the two black-clad women has its counterpart in the appearance and conduct of other characters Marlow encounters on his visit to the Company headquarters. His only memories of the secretary are a 'skinny forefinger' beckoning him into the next room, a 'white-haired . . . head' and a compassionate expression that seems to be as automatic as it is out of place. The 'great man' himself is, if anything, presented even more sketchily. His room (appropriately for that of someone whose dealings are with 'the Darkness') is dimly lit, and he himself (appropriately for one who functions at the heart of a 'whited sepulchre') is nothing more than an impression of 'pale plumpness'. His conversation is a vague murmur, his physical impact so indeterminate that Marlow remains unsure as to whether or not they shook hands. We are not told the precise position of this man who 'had his grip on the handle-end of ever so many millions', but there seems little doubt that Conrad intends us to see him as a prototypical director of companies. It should not pass unnoticed that one of his London counterparts is a member of Marlow's audience.

The shadowy figures of the secretary and the 'great man' serve to consolidate Marlow's unease – he is uncomfortable both with the formality of the interview and with having to sign 'some document' presented to him by the secretary – and the clerk and doctor, though both recognizably more human, do nothing to alleviate it. Rather the contrary. Both make it clear that they believe those who go 'out there' on the Company's business to be unhinged: the clerk is brutally direct, replying – when Marlow asks him why he does not make the trip himself – that he would not be so great a fool as to do so. The shabby old doctor is rather more circumspect: he obtains Marlow's leave to take detailed measurements of his skull and asks if there was ever any madness in his family. He comments on the 'mental changes' that inevitably affect those who go out to work in the Company's overseas stations, implying that if Marlow is not crazy now he surely will be before he returns to Europe.

The doctor's final advice is that his visitor 'avoid irritation more than exposure to the sun'. We wonder whether he ever offered the same counsel to Fresleven.

Disquiet over the undoubted physical dangers of his undertaking is, however, by no means Marlow's only worry. He is acutely conscious of the doubletalk that surrounds the Company's activities, and that things are not what they are made to seem. Even his good-natured aunt has been infected with the disease, having represented him – in order to secure his employment – as 'an exceptional and gifted creature'. The result is that he is now regarded 'as one of the Workers, with a capital ... Something like an emissary of light, something like a lower sort of apostle', ideally equipped to plunge into the darkness and wean 'the ignorant millions from their horrid ways'. That he realizes such quasi-religious imagery to be greatly misplaced, however, is clear from his venturing to hint to his aunt that the Company is actually run for profit. He feels himself to be an impostor. Certainly he is not the man his employers believe him to be, but he is also an impostor in the sense that he is playing a part – and, furthermore, doing so voluntarily – in the Company charade, while being under no illusions as to the nature and implications of that charade. No wonder that, albeit briefly, the physical discomforts that he is about to experience (at 'the centre of a continent') pale into insignificance beside the psychological hell ('the centre of the earth') to which – in going ahead with the venture – he is subjecting himself.

8. The Voyage Out (*pages 39–42*)

The voyage out enables Marlow to see the workings of the colonial system at first hand. The fact that he does so from the deck of a French steamer (calling at a seemingly endless string of French settlements) reflects its espousal by European powers both great and small during the second half of the nineteenth century. We are reminded of the map in the waiting room at the Company's headquarters, with its 'vast amount of red . . . a deuce of a lot of blue, a little green, smears of orange, and, on the East Coast, a purple patch'. Before his departure, Marlow may have had his suspicions about the gap between lofty ideals and practical realities; now he is able to confirm those suspicions for himself.

The coastline along which the ship makes its tedious way presents a far from attractive face. Bordered by an unending line of white surf that gives the impression of Nature herself trying to ward off intruders, it is 'almost featureless' and has an aspect of 'monotonous grimness'. All that can be made out from the sea is that the interior comprises one colossal jungle whose very profuseness – encouraged by fierce sun and high humidity – appears to threaten (it is 'so dark-green as to be almost black'). Nevertheless, like other coastlines the world over, it fascinates the traveller, seeming to whisper an invitation to 'Come and find out'. Closer inspection, however, confirms the distant impression: the river estuaries ('streams of death in life') into which they sail have banks 'rotting into mud', waters 'thickened into slime', mangroves that seem 'to writhe . . . in the extremity of an impotent despair'. Elsewhere, there is the 'still and earthy atmosphere as of an overheated catacomb', a fit setting for 'the merry dance of death and trade'. Throughout, we note the menace contained in the imagery.

The impact on this landscape of those bold enough to respond to its solicitations has been slight. Settlements that have been in existence for centuries are still 'no bigger than pinheads on the untouched expanse of their background'. Marlow's fellow-passengers, with whom – significantly – he feels himself to have no point of contact, are all soldiers or customs-officers, sent out with the express purpose of subduing one scrap of 'God-forsaken wilderness' or another, and exploiting it in the name of the mother-country. There is no evident concern for the well-being of these servants of the cause: some drown in the surf before even reaching shore, while those who make dry land are condemned to make some sort of lives for themselves in pretentiously-named clusters of tin sheds. Like the cheery-faced but naïve youths Marlow encounters at the Company's headquarters, they are dealt with anonymously and mechanically by an uncaring system: 'they were just flung out there, and on we went.'

A particular incident sums up the ineffectuality as well as the brutality of the typical colonial adventure. One day, the steamer passes a French man-of-war shelling the interior from her off-shore anchorage. Marlow is at a loss to know what she is in fact firing at, since 'there wasn't even a shed there'. The proceeding is marked by a profound lassitude, similar to that already observed in the Company's offices: the ship's ensign droops 'limp like a rag' and as the 'greasy, slimy swell' swings her lazily up and down, her thin masts sway to and fro. Moreover, all the proud declarations of colonial competence and enlightenment made in the board-rooms of European capitals are revealed as being, in reality, no more than hollow farce:

In the empty immensity of earth, sky, and water, there she was, incomprehensible, firing into a continent. Pop, would go one of the six-inch guns; a small flame would dart and vanish, a little white smoke would disappear, a tiny projectile would give a feeble screech – and nothing happened. (page 41)

Marlow is struck with the craziness of the operation, and is indignant when 'somebody on board' assures him that there is a camp of natives ('he called them enemies!') hidden in the bush. His indignation derives from his being able to observe for himself, on such occasions as they paddle their boats out to the steamer, the positive attributes of the country's black inhabitants, with their 'bone, muscle . . . wild vitality . . . intense energy of movement, that was . . . natural and true'. (We cannot miss the diametrical shift from its previously established associations of mystery and ignorance and evil that blackness undergoes at this point.) Unlike the Europeans, the natives 'wanted no excuse for being there'. As he looks at them, Marlow has the impression of being fully in touch with reality and experiences a surge of comfort. By comparison, the rest of his journey is 'like a weary pilgrimage amongst hints for nightmares'.

On arrival at the settlement – located at the mouth of the fascinating river – that serves as the territory's seat of government, he changes ships. The Swedish captain of the 'little sea-going steamer' he joins for the brief journey upstream to the Company Station manifests an undisguised contempt for government employees. By way of example of their lack – as a breed – of resource and staying power, he tells how, a few days earlier, he had taken up 'a man who hanged himself on the road'. As if to reinforce all the hints and warnings that Marlow has received to date, he speculates on the cause of the man's suicide: 'Who knows? The sun too much for him, or the country perhaps.'

9. First Impressions (*pages 42–5*)

If his voyage along the coast convinces Marlow of the ineffectuality of colonial enterprise, his arrival at the Company's Station quickly impresses him with its profligacy. The scene that confronts him is one of 'inhabited devastation'. Everywhere he walks his progress is impeded by some broken or abandoned object: a boiler wallows in the grass and a railway truck lies on its back 'as dead as the carcass of some animal', its three remaining wheels pointing uselessly to the sky. Machinery decays, nails are left to rust, imported drainage pipes intended for the improvement of conditions at the settlement are tumbled to their ruin down a narrow ravine. Such activity as there is strikes Marlow as both meaningless and wasteful:

A heavy and dull detonation shook the ground, a puff of smoke came out of the cliff, and that was all. No change appeared on the face of the rock. They were building a railway. The cliff was not in the way or anything; but this objectless blasting was all the work going on. (page 42)

Elsewhere, he comes upon a 'vast artificial hole' whose purpose he is unable to guess: 'It wasn't a quarry or a sandpit, anyhow. It was just a hole.' He indulges himself in the cynical surmise that it has something to do with the 'philanthropic desire' of keeping the natives occupied.

The natives, too, are everywhere Marlow turns, further examples of the Company's incompetent indifference. The first he encounters are shackled together and wear the iron collars of criminals. They are terribly emaciated, physically and psychologically overwrought, and are clothed in nothing but black rags. As they pass him, Marlow notes that they have the 'complete, deathlike indifference of unhappy savages'. They are guarded in their labours by another black, distinguished by a shabby uniform jacket and carelessly carried rifle. He is plainly 'one of the reclaimed, the product of the new forces at work', and he responds to the sight of Marlow ahead of him on the path with a speedy shouldering of arms and a 'large ... rascally grin' whose whiteness bespeaks a ready confederacy with his European masters. Marlow experiences a pang of discomfort at being associated in this way with the guard's ignominious office, but realizes that he can no longer be the detached observer that he was during the voyage out. 'After all,' he reflects bitterly, 'I also was a part of the great cause of these high and just

27

proceedings.' Another explosion from the railway excavations makes him think of the French warship shelling its 'enemies' in the empty bush. Now it is as if 'the outraged law' has come, in audible form and representing 'an insoluble mystery from the sea', to punish the natives – not for being flatly opposed to its demands – but for the crime of intractability, of being slow to learn.

On another occasion, intending to find a little shade, Marlow wanders into a grove seemingly filled with slowly dying men. It is as if he has stepped 'into the gloomy circle of some Inferno':

Black shapes crouched, lay, sat between the trees leaning against the trunks, clinging to the earth, half coming out, half effaced within the dim light, in all the attitudes of pain, abandonment, and despair. (page 44)

These men, he realizes, are neither enemies nor criminals, but legally indentured labourers who have been brought by a mindless system 'from all recesses of the coast' and are now being destroyed by a regimen of uncongenial surroundings and unfamiliar food. Their dehumanized condition is stressed by Marlow's description of them as 'bundles of acute angles', 'phantom[s]', 'creatures' and by his account of the way in which one of them is reduced to going 'on all fours towards the river' in order to get a drink.

As this section of the narrative proceeds, we become increasingly conscious of Conrad's questioning of the standard equation of white with good and black with bad. Nowhere is his manipulation of associations clearer than in Marlow's report of his brief encounter with one particular young negro in the same grove of death. Unaccustomed to the 'greenish gloom', he does not at first notice this parcel of 'black bones' lying only a few inches from where he is standing. As he watches, the man slowly turns his eyes towards him and he observes 'a kind of blind, white flicker in the depths of the orbs'. For a moment he is at a loss. Then, in an instinctive gesture of pity and humanity that sets him worlds apart from his fellow-whites, he offers the man a ship's biscuit that he happens to have in his pocket. Finally, he remarks the piece of white worsted that the man has tied round his neck: it looks startling and out of place against his black skin and Marlow wonders how it came there and what it means, if indeed it has any meaning. Significantly, his list of possibilities ends with the thought that it might be 'a propitiatory act' – that the man may be wearing it (and the fact that it is around his neck suggests a connection with the chain-gang and their iron collars) in order to appease his gods or his masters into some alleviation of his sufferings. Thus, in the course of this passage, white is primarily associated with blindness, indifference, exploitation and cruelty. In the exhausted and dying black workers, on the other hand, the reader cannot fail to find – like Marlow – a focus for his deepest compassion.

Such is Marlow's initiation into the ways of the Company Station. As he stands on the hillside overlooking the 'waste of excavations', he reflects on some of the faces of evil with which he has become familiar in the course of his various wanderings about the globe:

I've seen the devil of violence, and the devil of greed, and the devil of hot desire; but, by all the stars! these were strong, lusty, red-eyed devils, that swayed and drove men. (page 43)

Such were, however, infinitely more virile, more acceptable than the malign spirit whose work he recognizes as he gazes about him, the 'flabby, pretending, weak-eyed devil of a rapacious and pitiless folly'. It is a devil with whom he anticipates he will become even more closely acquainted as his tour of duty continues.

10. The Chief Accountant (*pages 45–7*)

Marlow's attitude to the first white man that he meets at the Company Station, the Chief Accountant – another figure with a specific London counterpart – is decidedly equivocal. At first, he sees him as something remarkable, an object of respect, a walking 'miracle' who is able to maintain both appearances and standards in spite of the demoralizing conditions under which he is obliged to live and work. Whiteness and precision radiate from his 'high starched collar . . . cuffs . . . light alpaca jacket, snowy trousers . . . clear necktie, and varnished boots'. His hair is 'parted, brushed, oiled' and he carries a parasol in his 'big white hand'. That he is said to have the 'appearance . . . of a hairdresser's dummy', however, suggests that there is also something artificial, something insubstantial about him. More importantly, he is a model of efficiency – a quality for which Marlow has already expressed his admiration – amid the pervasive muddle. His books, containing 'correct entries of perfectly correct transactions', are in apple-pie order. The moral impropriety of those transactions – the fact that 'a precious trickle of ivory' is paid for with 'rubbishy cottons, beads, and brass wire' – does not concern him. He is preoccupied with accuracy. He can accept the inadequacy of his surroundings – the 'narrow strips of sunlight' let in by the ramshackle construction of his office and falling across his back 'from neck to heels' remind us that he is, in his way, as much a prisoner of his circumstances as are the blacks on the chain-gang – so long as they do not interfere with the efficient performance of his duties. But when they do, he is quick to voice his impatience. The tumult of arrival and departure in the station yard occasions a characteristically unsympathetic comment: 'When one has got to make correct entries, one comes to hate those savages – hate them to death.' Nor is his annoyance confined to the 'violent babble' of the blacks: the groans of the dying agent, with whom he is required temporarily to share his office, 'distract [his] attention. And without that', he insists, 'it is extremely difficult to guard against clerical errors in this climate.' Efficiency, in the figure of the Chief Accountant, becomes synonymous with mechanical indifference to the lot of others.

It is the Accountant who also introduces Marlow to the name of Kurtz, the 'first-class' up-country agent whose main claim to fame is that he sends in from his one remote station as much ivory as all his

30

colleagues put together. There is, however, more to this man than an outstanding competence in carrying out the Company's mercantile objectives: he has, though we are not told precisely how or why, won the confidence of the Council in Europe. He is expected to go far, even perhaps to become 'somebody in the Administration'. The Accountant's enthusiasm for this 'very remarkable person' reminds us that Marlow, too, has been earmarked as 'an exceptional and gifted creature', one from whom the Company can expect great things. Kurtz, we gather, shares some of the Accountant's attitudes towards the efficient functioning of the Company. Marlow is asked, when he meets him, to assure Kurtz that 'everything here ... is very satisfactory'. The Accountant dare not write as much in a letter because he fears that it will fall into unsympathetic hands at the Central Station. We have only to think of the appalling waste of life, materials and human spirit that the Company Station stands for to appreciate the awful irony of his message.

11. The Overland Journey (*pages 47–9*)

The brief section of narrative that follows is concerned with Marlow's 'two-hundred-mile tramp', at the head of a column of sixty native porters, to the Company's Central Station where he is to join his command. The 'empty land' through which he passes is a model of inhospitality, its 'chilly ravines' alternating with 'stony hills ablaze with heat'. Most of all, however, he is struck by the intensity of the solitude, in which a total absence of population is counterpoised by the presence of a string of ruined and abandoned villages. His remark that 'the population had cleared out a long time ago' evokes the story of his predecessor, Fresleven, and we are led to wonder how often similar pointless dramas have been acted out in the relations of black and white. His understanding of the general situation is further demonstrated by his imagined transposition of the present circumstances, with 'a lot of mysterious niggers armed with all kinds of fearful weapons' suddenly taking to travelling back and forth along the road between Deal and Gravesend (placenames that, incidentally, suggest the relationship between commerce and death with neat precision), and 'catching the yokels right and left to carry heavy loads for them'. We are briefly reminded of his earlier evocation of the circumstances of the Roman colonization of the Thames estuary.

Marlow's only contacts with humanity during his journey are the occasional 'carrier dead in harness' and the drunken white man who claims to be responsible for the upkeep of the road. His comment is characteristic:

Can't say I saw any road or any upkeep, unless the body of a middle-aged negro, with a bullet-hole in the forehead . . . may be considered as a permanent improvement. (page 48)

While such remarks bespeak his continuing sensitivity towards the circumstances of his employment, Marlow is at the same time beginning to show signs – as he is himself aware – of undergoing certain of the 'mental changes' referred to, at the time of his visit to the 'whited sepulchre', by the Company's doctor. He complains of the 'exasperating habit' of his overweight travelling companion – a man who is prepared to be a burden to others as well as to himself in these alien surroundings out of sheer greed for financial gain – 'of fainting on the hot hillsides, miles away from the least bit of shade and water', and resents having to hold his own coat like a parasol over the man's head while he is coming round. He attempts – unsuccessfully as it turns out – to head off a mutiny among his bearers with a threatening speech accompanied by gestures, 'not one of which was lost on the sixty pairs of eyes' before him. It does not take much imagination to guess the import of his gestures, and – even if he has no intention whatsoever of carrying out his threats – we are reminded of the unfortunate negro who had somehow managed to cross the drunken roadmender. Certainly, by the time he hobbles with the remnants of his party into the Central Station, he feels distinctly that he is becoming 'scientifically interesting'.

33

12. The Central Station (*pages 49–59*)

The Central Station, when Marlow reaches it, proves to be as dismally unprepossessing as the Company Station, though for somewhat different reasons. It is situated on a backwater of the great river and bounded on one side by a stretch of 'smelly mud'. The rush fence designed to protect its other three flanks is in a state of tattered disrepair, while the only gate to the settlement is nothing but a 'neglected gap'. The white inhabitants of this outpost of progress seem to have little sense of purpose. They appear 'languidly' among the buildings, 'strolling up' to inspect the new arrival before retiring 'out of sight somewhere' as spiritlessly as they came. They have little or nothing worthwhile to occupy them: like the man appointed to make bricks but who cannot do so because he lacks some crucial but unspecified raw material, they are all 'waiting . . . for something'. They pass the time backbiting and engaging in pointless intrigues, their entire existence – 'the philanthropic pretence' of their enterprise, their 'talk . . . government . . . show of work' – being nothing but a sham. Like Marlow's companion on his journey from the Company Station, each lives for the day he will be appointed to a trading-post where he can make money. The 'absurd' long staves they carry everywhere as a mark of their authority – he even wonders with some amusement whether they take them to bed – make Marlow think of them as pilgrims, but pilgrims whose true faith has been bewitched out of them by the 'flabby . . . devil' of rapacity and replaced by worship of the material: 'The word "ivory" rang in the air, was whispered, was sighed. You would think they were praying to it' (page 52).

If this all seems ludicrous it also has distinctly sinister overtones: Marlow detects a taint in it 'like a whiff from some corpse'.

Life within the station has little contact with reality, which resides instead in the great, silent, mysterious landscape that surrounds it. Though Marlow is unable to plumb the meaning of this landscape, or determine whether its vast placidity is to be interpreted as an invitation or a threat, his every sense is alert to it and his descriptions of it have moments of powerful lyricism:

The great wall of vegetation, an exuberant and entangled mass of trunks, branches, leaves, boughs, festoons, motionless in the moonlight, was like a rioting invasion of soundless life, a rolling wave of plants, piled up, crested, ready to topple over the creek, to sweep every little man of us out of his little existence. And it moved not. (page 61)

He attempts to define his relationship (and that of the other whites) with this 'dumb thing': can they handle it, or are they fated to be 'handled', manipulated by it? He is, however, unable to come to any firm conclusion. He tries to picture what lies within it, but the facts and information he has at his disposal fail to produce any kind of image. The mystery remains.

Against the majesty of such a backdrop, human activity appears futile, peevish and, not infrequently, preposterous. The pilgrims' repeated efforts to dispose of the hippopotamus that makes a 'bad habit' of wandering through their encampment by night are a case in point: their turning out in force and emptying every available rifle in his general direction is a scaled-down version of the French man-of-war 'firing into a continent'. The sinking of the ship he has been sent out to command, two days before Marlow's arrival, is plainly an act of gross incompetence, but it is passed off by the 'excitable chap with black moustaches' as 'all right ... all quite correct', everyone involved having behaved 'splendidly'. This same man makes the identical comment – strongly reminiscent of that made by the Chief Accountant in describing the goings-on at the Company Station – when, one evening, a grass shed full of merchandise is disastrously destroyed by fire, while all the pilgrims seem capable of doing is 'cutting capers in the light, with their arms lifted high'. His own contribution on this occasion – carrying a quart of water from the river in a leaky bucket – is hardly more effectual. Such personal ineptitude does not, however, prevent his insisting on the severest measures being taken against the unfortunate black believed to have 'caused the fire in some way':

Transgression – punishment – bang! Pitiless, pitiless. That's the only way. This will prevent all conflagrations for the future. (page 55)

The hopeless incompetence of the whites might be mildly amusing were it not for the fact that it is unfailingly coupled with a blind and lethal ruthlessness.

13. The General Manager (*pages 50–52*)

The man who presides over the station's prevailing neglect and the lassitude and self-deception of its occupants is its unnamed General Manager. At first sight he seems merely unexceptional: we are told he is 'commonplace' in almost every respect (complexion, feature, manners, voice), that he is of 'middle' size and 'ordinary' build. His eyes are of the 'usual' blue. He is, indeed, a 'common trader' lacking any of the administrative qualities normally expected of someone in his position:

He had no genius for organizing, for initiative, or for order even . . . He had no learning, and no intelligence . . . He originated nothing, he could keep routine going – that's all. (page 50)

Marlow sums him up as a 'chattering idiot'. He does note, however, a certain coldness in the man's gaze from time to time and an indefinable expression about his lips, and comments that the only thing he inspires among those with whom he has dealings is uneasiness. He suspects that the Manager has risen to his present position through sheer staying power and for no better reason than that, unlike all the other whites, he never falls ill, commenting that 'triumphant health in the general rout of constitutions is a kind of power in itself'. He wonders what makes such a man tick and suggests that perhaps he has 'nothing within him'.

As if to confirm this and perhaps to offer some justification for his own inadequacies, the Manager is on record as believing that 'men who come out here should have no entrails'. There is no doubt that those who appear to cope most successfully with their environment have something of this quality: the Chief Accountant, for instance, reminds Marlow of 'a hairdresser's dummy' while the frustrated brickmaker is later described as a 'papier-mâché Mephistopheles' with 'nothing inside but a little loose dirt'. It is part of Conrad's intention that we understand the emptiness – the hollowness – of such men not just as some freak physical condition which puts them at an advantage over their fellow-whites, but – more crucially – as a metaphor for their moral and spiritual aridity. Marlow remarks that the Manager speaks and behaves as if he has 'a darkness . . . in his keeping'.

The agents of the Central Station obey their Manager but they do not respect him. This is in no way surprising because he fails utterly to rise

36

above the ethical level that they inhabit. While they connive against each other, he allows his black servant to treat them, 'under his very eyes, with provoking insolence', and is thought to employ one of their number to spy on them. He conspires in secret against Kurtz, while at the same time pretending huge admiration for the 'exceptional man', as well as concern enough for his health and safety to attempt the ill-advised and ultimately calamitous journey upriver in the steamer earmarked for Marlow's command.

His inefficiency and lack of concern are evident in his signal failure to procure the rivets necessary for the repair of the ship, in spite of Marlow's continued requests. Significantly, instead of rivets there comes 'an invasion, an infliction, a visitation'. The Eldorado Exploring Expedition, whose arrival causes 'the air of mystery [to] deepen a little over the muddle of the station', is led by the Manager's uncle, who seems to spend the entire space of his visit in prolonged and solitary conference with his nephew. Marlow's judgement on his superior is nowhere more positively implied than in his attitude to this enterprise in which the Manager has so close and profound (and, perhaps, financial) an interest. There is little of 'philanthropic pretence' about the venture, and the talk of its various members is like that of buccaneers: 'reckless without hardihood, greedy without audacity, and cruel without courage.' They have made no plans and there is no 'idea', no justification behind their intentions.

To tear treasure out of the bowels of the land was their desire, with no more moral purpose at the back of it than there is in burglars breaking into a safe. (page 61)

Such men must be seen, in the context of Marlow's earlier comments, as a living embodiment of the very worst aspects of colonial adventurism.

The General Manager is not, of course, alone among the characters and locations of *Heart of Darkness* in being identified by his function rather than by a proper name. Conrad made clear his reason for adopting this procedure in a letter to Richard Curle, in which he explained that – in his view – 'explicitness . . . is fatal to the glamour of all artistic work, robbing it of all suggestiveness, destroying all illusion.'[1] By suppressing proper names, he underscores the universal applicability of his themes: directors of companies inhabit the darkness that hovers over 'the biggest, and the greatest, town on earth' as well as the silent streets of the 'whited sepulchre', and the Accountant obliged to endure the inconveniences of life at the Company's Station has his counterpart aboard the *Nellie*. At the same time, the anonymity of the majority of characters highlights those few who are identified by name – most obviously Kurtz and Marlow himself – and focuses particular attention on their shared attributes.

14. The Brickmaker (*pages 53–9*)

This 'young aristocrat', with his forked beard and aquiline nose, is the General Manager's spy and co-conspirator. In the absence of materials essential to the carrying out of the task for which he has been appointed to the Central Station, he 'does secretarial work' for his superior. When Marlow hints that he might use this position to do something about the paralysing lack of rivets, he demonstrates his moral cowardice by insisting that he may write only what he is specifically directed to write. His caution is no doubt related to his ambition to rise to the rank of assistant-manager at the station, an aim in which he appears to have the Manager's support. He fears, however, that Kurtz – with his high reputation and the outstanding success he has enjoyed in the running of his own trading-post, the Inner Station – may well be promoted over him. These fears are augmented, furthermore, by the 'unfortunate accident' of the fire and the likelihood of its reflecting badly on the station's administration. It is while he is sharing his concerns on this issue with the General Manager that Marlow inadvertently interrupts them.

During his subsequent conversation with Marlow – in the course of which Marlow receives a strong impression that he is being pumped for information (or, at the very least, confirmation of existing suspicions) – the brickmaker reveals a bitter envy of Kurtz. He believes both his rival and Marlow to be favoured members of what he scathingly refers to as 'the new gang – the gang of virtue', from which he and his kind are positively excluded. When asked for a character of Kurtz he launches into a word-for-word recitation of sentiments he has seen expressed about the 'prodigy' in the Company's confidential correspondence (thus corroborating the Chief Accountant's suspicion that no messages sent by way of the Central Station are secure from prying eyes). Kurtz, unlike the average pilgrim – especially men like the Station Manager and his buccaneering uncle – is the epitome of those much prized 'European' qualities ('higher intelligence, wide sympathies, a singleness of purpose') for which the Company is anxious that its colonial enterprise gain a reputation in the world at large. He combines scientific knowledge and a striving after progress with compassion and humanity. He is destined to go far. As Marlow listens to the brickmaker, he is reminded of the fact that his own recruitment is also regarded as 'a piece of good fortune for

marlow is seen/comes to see himself?
as a younger Kurtz?

the Company', and his interest in and desire to meet the chief of the Inner Station begin to grow more pronounced:

> I was curious to see whether this man, who had come out equipped with moral ideas of some sort, would climb to the top after all and how he would set about his work when there. (page 62)

As for the brickmaker: for all his patent resentment of Kurtz, he is wary of crossing him. He makes a feeble attempt to persuade Marlow that his words are not to be interpreted in the way they may have seemed to be intended, that he does not wish to be 'misunderstood' or want Kurtz 'to get a false idea of [his] disposition'. The fact that he keeps, among the native trophies in his hut, a small sketch in oils made by Kurtz while he was waiting at the Central Station for transport upriver, suggests that he demonstrated a similar solicitousness in his first-hand dealings with the 'prodigy'.

Marlow gives a brief account of Kurtz's painting. It appears to be an allegorical subject: a 'draped and blindfolded' woman, carrying a lighted torch, moves in stately fashion against a sombre, 'almost black', background. Is she, perhaps, the figure of enlightened colonialism, bringing 'pity ... science ... progress' to the benighted masses? Her blindfold suggests impartiality, her stateliness the dignity of her undertaking. Such an interpretation would certainly square with what we have already learned of Kurtz's philosophy. There is, however, one discordant feature in the composition which does not escape Marlow's notice: 'the effect of the torch-light on the face was sinister.' Whether the face is only made to appear sinister by the play of the light or the light serves to reveal a sinisterness that has always been there, the suggestion of some hidden evil associated with the light-bringing process is unavoidable.

15. Marlow (*pages 56–62*)

Marlow's instinctive dislike for the brickmaker and growing sympathy for the unseen Kurtz are so strong that they bring him close to abandoning one of his most cherished principles, that of never telling a lie. For him, falsehoods have 'a taint of death, a flavour of mortality' – an expression similar to the one he uses to describe the all-pervasive ivory-worship, the living lie of the Central Station. However, as he listens to the jabber of his 'young fool' of an interlocutor, he determines to let him believe what he likes about the strength of his influence at the Company's European headquarters, about 'the powers' that have sent him out into the field:

I became in an instant as much of a pretence as the rest of the bewitched pilgrims. This simply because I had a notion it somehow would be of help to that Kurtz. (page 57)

There is very little in the derelict backwater of the Central Station with which Marlow feels in tune. The blacks are treated here no less cruelly than they are downriver; the rank-and-file white agents, lacking the will or the wherewithal to do anything constructive, pass their time in self-important bickering; and the Manager and his unofficial secretarial assistant – the only people with any influence at the station – are given to base plotting and empty chatter.

Marlow's chief source of comfort is, in fact, his damaged ship, which he refers to ironically as his 'influential friend', and there is powerful symbolism in 'that wretched, old, mangled steamboat' being at his back as he endures the brickmaker's conversation. He prefers to sleep aboard the vessel and chooses his friends from among the station mechanics ('despised' by the other whites 'on account of their imperfect manners') engaged in its repair. His own involvement in the refitting of the boat provides him with the much-needed opportunity to turn his back on the station and all that it stands for. It also enables him to keep a hold on what he refers to as 'the redeeming facts of life':

She had given me the chance to come out a bit – to find out what I could do. No, I don't like work. I had rather laze about and think of all the fine things that can be done. I don't like work, – no man does – but I like what is in the work, – the

41

chance to find yourself. Your own reality – for yourself, not for others – what no other man can ever know. They can only see the mere show, and never can tell what it really means. (pages 59–60)

His work on the vessel, in other words, gives Marlow an opportunity to demonstrate on a personal level the sort of devotion to efficiency about which he waxed eloquent in the course of his discussion of modern colonialism. It also provides the reader with a timely reminder that he is regarded by the Company administration as 'one of the Workers, with a capital', a special being, set apart from its other employees.

By this stage in *Heart of Darkness*, it has become clear to the reader that Marlow, as well as confronting the immediate difficulties of his physical journey, is also engaged in an extended spiritual pilgrimage or quest.[1] There is something about himself, his own 'reality', that he needs to find out, and it is rapidly becoming apparent to him that, in order to achieve this aim, he must – like visitors to the underworld in the ancient myths – seek the assistance of someone who knows and can speak the truth.[2] There is plainly no question of any kind of meaningful dialogue with the self-seeking, hypocritical pilgrims, but the likelihood of his learning something from Kurtz, the 'universal genius', increases as the days pass. Since Marlow needs a reliable means of transport in order to reach Kurtz at the Inner Station, his absorption in the repair of his steamboat becomes an integral part of the search for his own self.

It is at this stage that Marlow breaks off and speaks directly to his listeners aboard the *Nellie*. Are they able to penetrate his narrative, see where it is leading, understand its implications? He answers his own questions – or rather dismisses them as unanswerable – by suggesting an analogy between the experiences he is recounting and a dream, and by determining that 'no relation of a dream can convey the dream-sensation'. The reality of dreams is one in which absurdity, surprise and bewilderment are mingled in 'a tremor of struggling revolt'. Any attempt, furthermore, to relate that reality to the so-called reality of life is fraught with logical and philosophical as well as psychological difficulties. The intensely personal, even solitary, nature of dreams makes any attempt at their re-creation ultimately futile:

No, it is impossible; it is impossible to convey the life-sensation of any given epoch of one's existence – that which makes its truth, its meaning – its subtle and penetrating essence. It is impossible. We live, as we dream – alone . . . (page 57)

42

By now it is so dark aboard the *Nellie* that Marlow, sitting apart from his companions, is no longer visible to them. He has become a disembodied voice emerging from the blackness. In this he resembles Kurtz, who, at this point in the narrative, is still no more than an idea – 'a word' – that comes to him from somewhere in the darkness.

TRUTH IS

"The horror . . . The horror"

?

Part Two

16. The Conversation (*pages 63–6*)

The conversation between the General Manager and his uncle, which opens the second section of *Heart of Darkness*, serves two major purposes. The first of these is to provide the reader (and Marlow) with further information about the enigmatic Kurtz. The second is to demonstrate in some depth the cynicism that permeates the dealings of the Company and the attitudes of those in its employ.

We have already been made aware of the Manager's antagonism towards Kurtz and of his conniving with the brickmaker to bring about his promotion – at Kurtz's expense – to the position of assistant-manager at the Central Station. Now we learn that his dislike of Kurtz is as much rooted in the latter's autonomy as in the threat he offers to the brickmaker's ambitions. Kurtz has the ear of the Company's top administrators, who – impressed by his high ideals and fine rhetoric – have ignored the Manager's advice and ordered him to be posted to the Inner Station 'with the idea of showing what he [can] do'. The Manager mocks as 'pestiferous absurdity' what he has been obliged to hear of Kurtz's talk about 'humanizing, improving, instructing', convinced, as he is, that such matters have little to do with the harsh realities of management in the field. Ironically, however, he has – like the brickmaker – got Kurtz's words by heart.

The Manager also resents Kurtz's rejection of the assistant appointed to work with him and is stung by the suggestion that the 'poor devil' was sent to the Inner Station in a deliberate attempt to undermine him. The letter that the assistant brings from Kurtz on his return to the Central Station has a notably accusatory ring:

> Don't bother sending more of that sort. I had rather be alone than have the kind of men you can dispose of with me. (page 63)

Equally vexing to him is the fact that Kurtz has survived for more than a year without an officially-designated aide. Indeed, if his sending of a large, carefully documented consignment of prime ivory down the river in the unlikely care of a scoundrelly 'English half-caste clerk' is anything to go by, he has made something of a virtue of his solitariness.

His uncle expresses sympathy with the Manager's irritation by offering the hope that 'the climate may do away with this difficulty', that – in

47

other words – Kurtz may succumb, like so many of his predecessors, to the rigours of the environment. Exhorting his nephew to 'trust to this', he gestures with a 'black display of confidence' as if making some kind of pact with the wilderness. This 'treacherous appeal to the lurking death, to the hidden evil, to the profound darkness of its heart' is so startling to Marlow that he leaps to his feet, half expecting the forest to respond.

There have, indeed, been one or two – presumably gratifying – reports to suggest that all is not well with Kurtz. His sudden decision, after himself escorting the ivory shipment for three hundred miles of its journey down the river, to return to an Inner Station 'bare of goods and stores' in a small dugout canoe accompanied only by four native paddlers, seems astonishing and not a little crazy to both nephew and uncle. The fact that, according to the half-caste, Kurtz has been very ill and has recovered only 'imperfectly', finding it necessary to seek help from the doctor at a military post some way from his own station, also gives grounds for optimism. Finally, there has been no definite news of Kurtz for some nine months, only a number of 'strange rumours'. No white man has been anywhere near his district – except a 'pestilential' independent ivory trader, whose competition has been irritating the Company administration for some months and whom the Manager would dearly like to see hanged.

Aware of the jaundiced nature of the Manager's account, Marlow – whose concealment within spitting distance of the two speakers suggests his contempt for their opinions – is careful to reinterpret characters and events in his own mind. He recognizes the half-caste's achievement in conducting 'a difficult trip with great prudence and pluck' for what it really is. (Though he does not develop the notion at this point, there is clear evidence elsewhere in his narrative that Marlow regards a character's English background or training as – to some extent – guaranteeing his moral and intellectual rectitude. No doubt we are intended to understand the half-caste's accomplishment as having its basis in his Englishness.) Similarly, Kurtz's odd and inexplicable return to his 'empty and desolate' post assumes, for him, the aspect of a deed of heroism –

the lone white man turning his back suddenly on the headquarters, on relief, on thoughts of home – perhaps; setting his face towards the depths of the wilderness. (page 64)

It is not, perhaps, too fanciful to wonder in the same way what the itinerant ivory trader, whom the Manager so much despises, might really be like. Marlow, unfortunately, does not share in our conjecture.

In contrast to the half-caste and Kurtz, the Manager and his uncle are

– in Marlow's eyes – inferior and unworthy figures: he draws attention to the latter's short, flipper-like arm and – in a phrase which he is to use again at an important juncture later in *Heart of Darkness* – alludes to the presence of the two men as a 'fantastic invasion' of the high stillness of forest and river. The evening light is particularly effective in exposing their impotent grotesquery:

The sun was low; and leaning forward side by side, they seemed to be tugging painfully uphill their two ridiculous shadows of unequal length, that trailed behind them slowly over the tall grass without bending a single blade. (pages 65–6)

It comes as little surprise for the reader to learn, in the very next paragraph, of the failure of the uncle's Eldorado Expedition. Such men may strike dramatic postures against the wilderness backdrop, but they are totally unable to enter into any kind of relationship with it.

unlike Kurtz

because evil pacts with wilderness etc comes from colonialism / Europe.

Kurtz sees the evil darkness comes from Europe

17. The River Journey (*pages 66–70*)

Manoeuvring his 'tin-pot steamboat' upstream toward the Inner Station, Marlow experiences the 'high stillness of primeval forest' at first hand. The setting his words evoke is alien and uninviting: it is, indeed, an 'empty' . . . silent . . . 'impenetrable' . . . joyless . . . 'deserted' . . . gloomy . . . 'vengeful' place. He has the sensation of 'travelling back to the earliest beginnings of the world', of 'taking possession of an accursed inheritance' which is only to be brought under control at the expense of 'profound anguish and . . . excessive toil'. Wooded islands, that on another river might be welcomed as familiar landmarks, here 'mob' his vessel, which consequently loses its way and finds itself constantly 'butting . . . against shoals', everlastingly negotiating treacherous shallows in an effort to guess a way into the right channel. Marlow admits to a sense of powerlessness, to feeling like 'a blindfolded man set to drive a van over a bad road', and acknowledges that it is, for the most part, luck rather than judgement that gets the boat past the various hidden banks and 'sly old snag[s]' that lie in its way.

He is once again reminded of the similarity of his experience to a dream – the kind in which the dreamer experiences a sensation of hopeless disorientation, of being separated from reality: in which 'you thought yourself bewitched and cut off for ever from everything you had known once – somewhere – far away – in another existence perhaps' (page 66). It is at such moments of living dream, when he is so preoccupied with the business of navigation that he barely has time to think, that he finds images and memories from his past coming unbidden into his consciousness. They, too, come 'in the shape of an unrestful and noisy dream', so that the total effect is of one dream, with all its arbitrariness and incoherence, existing within the borders of another. Ever-present, furthermore, both within (and part of) the dream-complex, and also outside (and thus an alternative to) it, is the wilderness, which Marlow conceives of as an animate being with its own meanings and its own designs. The power of this being is conveyed strikingly in the image of the forest stepping leisurely across the water after the boat has passed 'to bar the way for our return'. Its stillness is that 'of an implacable force brooding over an inscrutable intention'. Marlow is, however, no nearer deciphering that intention now than he was during his moonlit conversation with the brickmaker at the Central Station.

Typically, he is rescued from the discomfort of his uncertainty as to whether the wilderness means well or harm to him and his companions, whether its stillness is to be read 'as an appeal or as a menace,' by his responsibilities as skipper. 'When you have to attend to things of that sort,' he comments, 'to the mere incidents of the surface, the reality – the reality I tell you – fades. The inner truth is hidden – luckily, luckily' (page 67). Nevertheless, he remains ever conscious of the mysterious presence watching him at his 'monkey tricks'. He develops the fairground image, suggesting that he is not alone in ignoring reality for the sake of more trivial, eye-catching preoccupations. The professional men in his audience aboard the *Nellie*, labourers within the 'brooding gloom' of London, are as much absorbed in the 'mere show' of life as he, though he concedes that there is perhaps a greater element of risk involved in balancing on a high wire than there is dancing atop a barrel-organ.

Such 'tricks' as performing first aid on the steam-pipes with 'whitelead and strips of woollen blanket', gathering dead wood for use as the next day's fuel, keeping an eye on the steering and 'circumventing those snags' also provide a distraction for Marlow from other more 'creepy thoughts'. These have to do with what he perceives to be his relationship with the natives whose settlements they pass from time to time on the banks of the river. At first these people remind us of the coast-dwellers who paddled their canoes through the surf to meet the ship on its journey out from Europe. There is a natural and comforting vitality about them which contrasts strongly with the shabby lethargy of the whites:

there would be a glimpse of rush walls, of peaked grass-roofs, a burst of yells, a whirl of black limbs, a mass of hands clapping, of feet stamping, of bodies swaying, of eyes rolling. (page 68)

Marlow's admiration is, however, tinged with puzzlement. What does all this activity signify? Once again he feels isolated from reality by a lack of 'comprehension of [his] surroundings'. The ship and its passengers glide past as if in a dream, 'like phantoms' that have long since left this primitive world behind and that can no longer remember anything about it.

Nevertheless, his attitude to the 'black and incomprehensible frenzy' he witnesses is sympathetic as well as merely interested. He is 'thrilled' by the thought of what he has in common with the dancers, of his 'remote kinship with this wild and passionate uproar'. Nor does he believe his feelings to be in any way idiosyncratic or odd:

if you were man enough you would admit to yourself that there was in you just the faintest trace of a response to the terrible frankness of that noise, a dim suspicion of there being a meaning in it which you . . . could comprehend. (page 69)

Even though he is unable to say exactly what the meaning of the dancing is ('joy, fear, sorrow, devotion, valour, rage – who can tell?'), he cannot fail to respond in some sort to its vigorous humanity. Its truth calls out to his being from 'the night of first ages', appealing to the primal instincts that he shares with the rest of mankind, tempting him towards atavistic reversion. It takes a substantial measure of self-restraint, he realizes, a strong personality and 'a deliberate belief' to resist such an appeal. 'Principles . . . acquisitions, clothes'– the patina of civilization – are not enough. In the event, however, it is his practical responsibilities aboard the steamer rather than fine but unspecified sentiments that prevent his going ashore to join the natives 'for a howl and a dance'.

This tension in Marlow's attitude towards such of the native life as he is able to glimpse from the decks of his steamboat is matched by an ambivalence towards the blacks under his command. While, on the one hand, he frankly admits his gratitude to them and admits that they are 'men one [can] work with', on the other, his uncomfortable little joke about their not actually eating one another in front of his face smacks more than a little of moral, if not racial, superiority. Their acknowledged practical usefulness in pushing the grounded boat out of a succession of shoals is mitigated by mention of the 'splashing around' that seems to be an unavoidable part of the operation. The real giveaway, however, comes – as Chinua Achebe points out[1] – in Marlow's condescending assertion that cannibals are fine enough fellows 'in their place' and in his sardonic description of 'the savage' who acts as the vessel's fireman. This man is patently *not* in his place: he bears all the outward signs of his own culture – teeth filed, hair shaved into patterns, cheeks ritually scarred, lip pierced and decorated – and ought to be 'clapping his hands and stamping his feet on the bank'. He has, however, undergone months of so-called 'improvement' at the hands of the Company and is able, as a result, to carry out a few simple technical operations. That Marlow sees such improvement for the deleterious process that it is, is suggested by his analogy of 'a dog in a parody of breeches and a feather hat, walking on his hind-legs'. His doubtless genuine sympathy for this 'poor devil' is, however, undermined by the condescending manner he adopts to describe the man's limited understanding of the duties he has to perform. The racist overtone of his references to the fellow's 'evident effort of intrepidity' in examining the gauges, his being 'a thrall to strange witch-craft' which has provided him with 'improving knowledge', and his belief that there is a potentially thirsty evil spirit lurking within the boiler, ready to wreak its vengeance on him if he fails to keep it properly stoked, all put Marlow at a greater distance from his subject than we might have expected from our reading of *Heart of Darkness* up to this point. Such distancing is perhaps inevitable, however, when one culture is viewed through the eyes of another, when European perceptions in all their narrowness are allowed to range freely over the unfamiliar territory of African conduct and custom.

If, at this point in the second section of the novella, Marlow's perception of the blacks he encounters is seen to become increasingly complex, the same is not true of his view of his fellow-whites. The 'three or four pilgrims' that – together with the Manager – are making the journey upriver still sport their staves and the attitudes that go with them ('all complete'), still seem to have little notion of the realities of their existence. They travel on the 'little begrimed steamboat' without much understanding of where it is taking them, except that it is a place, they hope, where they can make money. The agents who inhabit the scattered riverside outposts, moreover, live – like their colleagues at the Central Station – in tumbledown squalor, apparently held to their posts 'captive by a spell', perennially devoted to the worship of ivory.

18. The Deserted Settlement (*pages 70–72*)

Marlow's account of the scene at the deserted settlement that the travellers come upon some fifty miles short of the Inner Station provides a further instance of how imported perceptions can be deeply misleading. The main impression he conveys is of an inexplicable contradictoriness. He remarks the discrepancy between general ruin (the dismantled hut with its 'torn curtain of red twill' flapping sadly in the doorway, its primitive furniture and heap of rubbish; the 'inclined and melancholy pole' from which fly the tatters of some kind of flag) and careful provision (the 'neatly stacked' pile of wood; the 'lovingly' and, apparently, recently stitched binding of Towson's *Inquiry*); between the urgency of the message and the faded inadequacy of the medium in which it is conveyed; between the exhortation to hurry and the admonition to exercise caution. He makes no effort to envisage the reasons for these contradictions, but assesses the scene – as he assesses the native Africans – entirely from his own blinkered viewpoint. Accordingly, he joins his companions in blaming the elusive message for the 'imbecility of [its] telegraphic style'; decides – on the strength, presumably, of the message and the Towson book – that the former occupant of the hut must be English; and comes to the conclusion that, because he cannot read the book's pencilled marginalia, they must be written in cipher.

This sort of contradictoriness is, of course, perfectly consonant with the dream-quality of Marlow's experiences in general, a truth of which we are reminded when he remarks about the book that 'the simple old sailor ... made me forget the jungle and the pilgrims in a delicious sensation of having come upon something unmistakably real' (page 71). Ironically, this book provides Marlow with a useful lesson – though he does not seem to register the fact – on the deceptiveness of appearances and the care required in their interpretation. On the outside, it is an 'amazing antiquity' which he feels constrained to handle with the 'greatest possible tenderness'. When he opens it, however, it seems 'dreary reading enough', with its diagrams and 'repulsive tables of figures'. He notes the author's earnest interest in such matters as 'the breaking strain of ships' chains and tackle' and declares that it is 'not a very enthralling book'. He then, of course, proceeds to become so wrapped up in it that he neglects his duty of supervising the transfer of the wood to the steamer, and is only shaken out of his preoccupations by the sound of the Manager, 'aided by all the pilgrims', shouting at him from the riverbank. Once the boat is under way again, the Manager – deliberately ignoring the goodwill and helpfulness intended by both wood-pile and message – gives voice to the supposition that the settlement has something to do with the 'miserable trader' whose activities have been causing the Company so much grief, and about whom he complained to his uncle in the course of their secret, moonlight conversation. His remark both confirms our view of the Manager's mean-spiritedness and makes us (and, perhaps, Marlow) all the more anxious to see for ourselves what this man is really like.

19. Events in the Fog (*pages 72–8*)

As the journey continues, Marlow becomes increasingly more anxious to meet Kurtz. The decrepitude of the steamer and the power of the opposing current, however, mean that progress is slowed almost to a snail's-pace and his patience is sorely taxed. He takes to considering how much – if anything – of what he has heard or overheard at the Central Station he should pass on to Kurtz:

> But before I could come to any conclusion it occurred to me that my speech or my silence, indeed any action of mine, would be a mere futility. (page 72)

It seems to him that little of any consequence will be effected by a change of manager. In a moment of uncharacteristic resignation he admits that 'the essentials of this affair' lie beyond his reach, beyond his power of meddling. Though he does not himself make the connection, it is worth noting that one of the most common of dream-sensations is a feeling of inadequacy, of powerlessness in the face of some significant challenge or danger.

Marlow's impatience reaches a peak when, towards the evening of the second day, the boat is some eight miles from its destination. Such is his anxiety to press on that he momentarily forgets the warning message on the wood-pile. It is left to the Manager to remind him of it and point out that it would be most unwise to attempt the difficult stretch of river that they are about to enter in the gathering dark. Marlow acknowledges the sense of this argument and concedes that his annoyance at the inevitable delay lacks reasonableness. That he should have to be taught his craft by someone whose mediocrity and incompetence he has been at pains to emphasize earlier in his narrative is an indication of the degree to which he – like everyone else – has been adversely influenced by circumstances and surroundings. The balance is restored the next day when, in reply to the Manager's suggestion that – in spite of obvious dangers – they press on to the Inner Station, Marlow firmly asserts his refusal to take any risks.

Impatience turns to deep uneasiness when dawn comes and the boat is discovered to be shrouded in an impenetrable and unmoving blanket of fog, whose whiteness, significantly, makes it 'more blinding than the night'. There is a disquieting unnaturalness about the way it lifts and descends like 'a shutter . . . sliding in greased grooves'. What unnerves the travellers more than the fog, however, is the coincidence of 'a cry, a very loud cry, as of infinite desolation', followed by a 'tumultuous and mournful uproar' that seems to come at them from all sides at once. It is – to Marlow's way of thinking – as if the mist itself is screaming, as if it and whatever is happening ashore have somehow become one. And the thought makes his scalp creep.

Practical considerations, as always, bring him back to present reality and he gives instructions for the boat to be made ready for a quick getaway. He also takes a moment to stand back a little from the situation, to observe the reactions of the pilgrims both to the outburst from the shore and also the 'appalling and excessive silence' that follows it, and contrast them with those of the boat's native crew. The whites variously stammer, murmur or quarrel in hurried whispers. They gape, open-mouthed, and dart scared glances. Faces twitch with strain, eyes stare in unblinking fear, hands tremble. Two of the men rush to the cabin for their Winchesters. In addition to their general disquiet, Marlow notes that 'the whites . . . [have] . . . a curious look of being painfully shocked by such an outrageous row'.

The blacks, on the other hand, appear alert and interested, though not unduly excited; they grin and converse with each other briefly. Marlow plainly feels more at one with them, under the present circumstances, than with his fellow-whites. He alludes to the striking appearance of their broad-chested young headman, noting the way in which he gazes out into the fog 'in a dignified and profoundly pensive attitude'. It is to this man, not to the Manager or some other pilgrim, that Marlow turns to speak 'for good fellowship's sake'. And when, in return, the request is made that any prisoners taken in the coming skirmish be handed over to the natives for food, he swallows his 'proper' abhorrence and proceeds to make excuses for them. Their hunger is, after all, a direct consequence of the Company's failure to make adequate provision; of the European wisdom that with great punctiliousness pays each of them 'every week three pieces of brass wire, each about nine inches long' with which to purchase supplies at river-side villages that, in the event, prove to be non-existent or hostile or too bothersome – at least in the Manager's view – to stop at; and of the unilateral disposal by the pilgrims, 'in the midst of a shocking hullabaloo', of such supplies of rotten hippo-meat as the natives had brought along with them.

Here as in his earlier descriptions, however, we detect some ambivalence (though it may well not be conscious) in Marlow's attitude to his native crew. This emerges most clearly in his gratuitous remarks about their not having 'any clear idea of time' and in his record of and reference to their mode of speech. His monosyllabic utterance, for example, accompanied by the almost inevitable 'bloodshot widening of his eyes and ... flash of sharp teeth', turns the impressive-looking headman at a stroke into a caricature semi-articulate black. This, as Achebe points out,[1] is one of only two occasions in the whole of *Heart of Darkness* when Marlow records the actual words spoken by native characters. For the rest of the time, he is content to refer, vaguely and chauvinistically, to their 'violent babble of uncouth sounds' or, as here, to their exchange of 'short, grunting phrases' – thus denying them the dignity of intelligent expression, if not positively reducing them to the level of animals.

His discussion of the crew members' predicament over food leads Marlow to wonder why, the pressures on them being what they are, they have not turned on their white employers:

Why in the name of all the gnawing devils of hunger they didn't go for us – they were thirty to five – and have a good tuck in for once, amazes me now when I think of it. (page 75)

They are, after all, 'big powerful men', courageous, strong; and they have the advantage of a diminished capacity to weigh the consequences of their actions. The only answer that he can come up with is that 'something restraining, one of those human secrets that baffle probability, had come into play there'. He is, however, entirely at a loss to pinpoint the exact identity of the restraining force: 'was it superstition, disgust, patience, fear – or some kind of primitive honour?' He dismisses each of these options in turn, commenting that, in his own experience, it is easier to withstand bereavement, dishonour, even soul's perdition, than the terrible power of prolonged hunger.

And these chaps, too, had no earthly reason for any kind of scruple. Restraint! I would just as soon have expected restraint from a hyena prowling amongst the corpses of a battlefield. (page 76)

His puzzlement is aggravated, no doubt, by the fact that it was – as we have seen – practical preoccupations rather than 'fine sentiments' that prevented his being lured ashore, somewhat earlier, by the prospect of 'a howl and a dance'. Finally, however, he is obliged to accept the cannibals' restraint as a fact, but one so baffling that it supersedes and distracts his attention from the 'curious, inexplicable note of desperate grief in [the] savage clamour that had swept by us on the river-bank'.

20. Marlow's Errors of Judgement (*pages 77–9*)

Before the steamboat arrives at its destination, Marlow is responsible for two important errors of judgement. The more critical of these relates to the attack which he – unlike everyone else on board – is convinced is not going to take place. Ironically, he makes this particular blunder just after he has quite properly refused to respond to the Manager's rash suggestion that – the fog notwithstanding – he get the vessel under way again. He has no difficulty in seeing through his superior's feigned concern for Kurtz; nor is he taken in by the Manager's over-civil deference to his own authority as captain. It is perhaps natural, therefore, that at this particular moment his pronouncements on the matter of the attack should have a markedly self-confident ring. The fog, he points out, is the first reason for assuming themselves safe (in this prediction he is, of course, correct, but he does not consider the broader possibility of an attack once the fog has lifted); the second is the impenetrability of the jungle foliage on the riverbanks which makes the launching of canoes difficult, if not impossible (he does not, apparently, suspect that an assault might be mounted from the banks themselves); the third reason, and the real clincher, is the nature of that noise, those cries from beyond and within the blinding fog, which do not – to his ears – suggest 'immediate hostile intention'.

Unexpected, wild, and violent as they had been, they had given me an irresistible impression of sorrow. The glimpse of the steamboat had for some reason filled those savages with unrestrained grief. (page 78)

The only danger threatening the party is, he feels, its proximity to 'a great human passion let loose'. (As we later discover, this hypothesis is also correct, though, in the final analysis, the effects of 'a great human passion let loose' and aggressive intent turn out to be identical. Marlow, throughout, stubbornly maintains that the attack's protective purpose and the fact that it is 'undertaken under the stress of desperation' make it more accurately described as 'an attempt at repulse'.) Not content with confiding his views to the Manager alone, Marlow delivers 'a regular lecture' on the subject to the bemused pilgrims. Significantly, although he counsels the 'dear boys' against 'bothering', he continues himself to 'watch the fog for the signs of lifting as a cat watches a mouse'.

That Marlow is not necessarily to blame for this particular error of judgement is made clear by the nature of his second miscalculation. This concerns his choice of channel for the final approach to the Inner Station, a choice made on the basis of an imperfect understanding of his surroundings but in full awareness of how unreliable it is possible for first impressions to be. His narrative at this point is an excellent illustration of the stages by which an observer comes to realize the difference between what he thinks he sees from a distance and what, on closer examination, emerges as the reality. It also provides a model dissection of the workings of what commentators have long recognized as an important impressionist element in Conrad's writing.[1]

One of the principal aims of the painters of the late nineteenth-century Impressionist movement was faithfully to reproduce what they saw rather than what they knew to exist. A distant steeple half-obscured by driving rain was to be depicted as the uncertain smudge registered by the eye, not the solid architectural feature rationalized by the intellect. Put another way, the Impressionists were interested not so much in painting the fact of a steeple as in conveying its effect. In Marlow's description, we are guided through the process by which unclear effect is slowly focused into sharp fact.

About a mile and a half below the station, the steamboat rounds a bend giving on to a straightish reach of water. Some way off, in the middle of the stream, Marlow notices 'an islet, a mere grassy hummock of bright green', which, as he approaches it, turns out to be 'the head of a long sandbank'. He is able to refine his definition even further as a result of more immediate inspection, deciding that it is actually 'a chain of shallow patches stretching down the middle of the river'. Even this revised impression, however, is not to be his final word on the subject. From his elevated viewpoint on the cabin roof, he sees that these patches are strung out in a very particular way: 'exactly as a man's backbone is seen running down the middle of his back under the skin'. The enormous difference, demonstrated here, between the distant effect and the closely scrutinized fact, between initial idea and eventual understanding, is a central concern in *Heart of Darkness*. We are reminded of the occasions, earlier in the story, when distance had given Marlow the feeling of being cut off from reality.

We are clearly intended to interpret what comes next in Marlow's account in the light of this preparatory analysis, his choice of words constantly reminding us of the potentially misleading nature of appearances:

Now, *as far as I did see*, I could go to the right or to the left of [the shoals]. *I didn't know* either channel, of course. The banks *looked* pretty well alike, the depth *appeared* the same; but as *I had been informed* the station was on the west side, I naturally headed for the western passage. (pages 78–9, my italics)

As soon as he enters this western passage, however, he realizes that, once again, his eyes have deceived him. It turns out to be much narrower than he supposed and he is forced to seek the deep water close beneath the 'heavily overgrown' bank. It is while he is attempting to negotiate his vessel through these awkward circumstances that the unexpected attack 'develop[s] itself'.

21. The Attack (*pages 79–82*)

Marlow's narration of the attack employs an impressionistic method closely similar to the one adopted in his description of the shoals: in it, that is to say, the presentation of happenings and sensations is detached from – and in chronological terms precedes – the revelation of their true significance. Marlow follows this particular line of approach in the relating of three distinct occurrences.

The first of these takes as its starting point his preoccupation with the increasing shallowness of the channel through which the boat is sailing. From his perch 'on the extreme fore-end' of the cabin roof he watches 'one of [his] hungry and forebearing friends' manipulating the sounding-pole below him. Suddenly, to his utter amazement, the man 'give[s] up the business ... and stretch[es] himself flat on the deck, without even taking the trouble to haul his pole in'. What, in other words, Marlow sees is a shiftless black taking an unauthorized break from his duties. The poleman's laziness, moreover, is catching:

At the same time the fireman, whom I could also see below me, sat down abruptly before his furnace and ducked his head. (page 80)

The ducking of the fireman's head does not, of course, entirely harmonize with the general pattern of Marlow's observations, but he is denied the leisure to sharpen his focus by the appearance of a snag directly in the vessel's path. Concentrating his attention on this new danger, as his seaman's training and position of command have naturally conditioned him to do, he does not for the moment make anything of the fact that harmless-looking 'little sticks' have started 'flying about' in all directions. Only when the boat has – albeit clumsily – cleared the snag does his mind convert sensory effect into comprehended fact: 'Arrows, by Jove! We were being shot at!'

The second occurrence concerns Marlow himself much more nearly, and the very terms in which he explains it are highly suggestive of the impressionistic method. Having now achieved a fuller perception of what is going on around him, he leans 'right out' in order to close the shutter on the shoreward side of the cabin. As he does so, he sees a face, on a level with his own, looking at him from amongst the foliage on the riverbank. Though it looks at him 'very fierce and steady', it holds for the moment no special meaning or significance, being nothing more than an image, an appearance. Suddenly, however, his gaze takes him beyond the face and he is aware, 'deep in the tangled gloom', of 'naked breasts, arms, legs, glaring eyes'. The impression like a later one in his account of the attack, when he sees 'vague forms of men running bent double, leaping, gliding, indistinct, incomplete, evanescent' is highly fragmented and allusive. Nevertheless, it has the effect of clarifying for him the meaning of that single face. It is, to use Marlow's own simile, as if a veil has been removed from his eyes.

Marlow's description of the third and final occurrence is the most detailed and extended of all. Having taken over the steering of the steamboat because its 'fool-nigger' of a helmsman has deserted his post, has thrown the shoreward shutter back open and is even now, in emulation of the panic-stricken pilgrims, firing the Martini-Henry blindly into the bush, Marlow finds himself suddenly obliged to throw back his head and take evasive action as 'a glinting whizz' traverses the pilot-house, 'in at one shutterhole and out at the other'. He is more able to put a name to the object that produces this effect than he is to the 'something big' that appears 'in the air before the shutter' a few seconds later. When, furthermore, the various occurrences observed by Marlow subsequent to the arrival of the second object shape themselves into some sort of meaning (the helmsman drops the rifle, steps back swiftly, looks round at Marlow 'in an extraordinary, profound, familiar manner' before falling at his feet, hitting the side of his head against the wheel twice in the process; simultaneously, what appears to be a long cane clatters around the pilot-house and knocks over a small camp-stool) it turns out to be entirely the wrong meaning:

It looked as though after wrenching that thing from somebody ashore [the helmsman] had lost his balance in the effort. (page 81)

His error derives, as in the case of the arrows, from the fact that Marlow is more immediately concerned with the safe negotiation of his vessel past the snags that continue to crop up in its path. It is only the vivid and unlikely sensation of his feet feeling 'very warm and wet' that causes him to look down and understand the precise facts of the matter:

The man had rolled on his back and stared straight up at me; both his hands clutched that cane. It was the shaft of a spear that, either thrown or lunged through the opening, had caught him in the side just below the ribs; the blade had gone in out of sight, after making a frightful gash; my shoes were full; a pool of blood lay very still, gleaming dark-red under the wheel; his eyes shone with an amazing lustre. (pages 81–2)

In spite of the clarity and forcefulness of this particular revelation, it is interesting to see how Marlow persists, in his account of the episode, in describing – if not perceiving – the real in terms of the imaginary. The helmsman's anxious gaze combined with his firm grip on the spear, for example, give the appearance of his being afraid that he is about to be forcibly deprived of his prize – an effect closely related to Marlow's original mistaken impression that the man had lost his balance while 'wrenching that thing from somebody ashore'. A little later, his 'lustrous and inquiring glance' almost brings Marlow to the belief that the dying man is capable of speaking 'in an understandable language'.

Earlier in *Heart of Darkness* Marlow has made it clear, as we have seen, that only solid, factual objects and preoccupations – the damaged steamboat and its repair, the exigencies of navigation, Towson's *Inquiry* – can provide him with the defence necessary against the unhealthy fascinations of native life on the one hand, and the dream-delusions of colonialism on the other. He emphasizes that only by clinging to what is 'real' can he avoid being drawn into the fantasy. The narrative method he adopts in his account of the attack on the steamboat now implicitly suggests that one order of reality can conceal another from even the most practised of observers, that the honest immediacy of duty can obscure the actuality of arrows, enemies and men falling dead on all sides. In doing so, it calls into question the very nature of human experience, of our perception of what is real and what is appearance, what is fact and what is dream. And, on a broader scale, it reminds us that truth is a relative rather than an absolute commodity.

22. Marlow's Digression:
The Character of Kurtz (*pages 82–8*)

Up to this point, Marlow has preserved a careful chronology in his narration of detail and events, even down – as we have seen – to the precise sequence in which individual sensations presented themselves to him. In particular, he has told his audience no more about Kurtz than he has himself from time to time heard. He has, indeed, maintained the tension of his narrative by periodically voicing his pleasurable anticipation of conversation with the chief of the Inner Station, a man with whom, of all those he has encountered during his 'fresh-water' adventure, he senses that he has something in common. Now, however, he departs from this procedure to embark on a lengthy reflection – one whose rather discursive and fragmented nature once again suggests the workings of dreams – on aspects of Kurtz's behaviour and personality about which he is to glean information only later in the story.

His cue for this digressive leap forward is his brief conversation with 'the pilgrim in pink pyjamas' as they stand over the body of the unfortunate helmsman:

'He is dead,' murmured the fellow, immensely impressed. 'No doubt about it,' said I . . . 'And by the way, I suppose Mr Kurtz is dead as well by this time.' (page 82)

Marlow gives no reasons for this conjecture – one, incidentally, in which he again turns out, as he immediately admits, to be wrong – though his judgement is doubtless affected by the inordinate slowness of their progress upriver and what he interprets as the 'utter despair' of Kurtz's natives at their arrival in the vicinity of the Inner Station. Whatever its basis, it remains, for the moment, his 'dominant thought'. He employs a typical dream-reference to register his extreme disappointment: it is 'as though I had found out I had been striving after something altogether without a substance'. He comes to the 'strange discovery' that he has, all along, been thinking of Kurtz (in spite of his much envied practical success as one of the Company's outstanding field representatives) not so much as an agent, one who does things, but as a speaker or even – less substantially – as that speaker's disembodied voice. He no longer thinks so much in terms of seeing Kurtz or shaking him by the hand, as of hearing him. And just as, as an agent, Kurtz has the reputation of employing unscrupulous and illegal methods in his quest for ivory, so, as a voice, he must as surely be a vehicle of evil as he is one of good. In a passage of great lyric power, Marlow hints for the first time that the man he will meet at the end of his lengthy and arduous journey is not the wholly admirable figure that he has hitherto been painted:

> The point was in his being a gifted creature, and that of all his gifts the one that stood out pre-eminently, that carried with it a sense of real presence, was his ability to talk, his words – the gift of expression, the bewildering, the illuminating, the most exalted and the most contemptible, the pulsating stream of light, or the deceitful flow from the heart of an impenetrable darkness. (page 83)

The conviction that such a voice should be silenced without his having the opportunity to listen to what it has to say fills Marlow with a feeling of 'lonely desolation'. He is cut to the quick, admitting – without shame, though to the utter incredulity of at least one of his listeners – to the exhibition of his sorrow in 'a startling extravagance of emotion', a direct and notable counterpart of that displayed by the 'savages in the bush'. He can no more restrain himself, under the circumstances, than can they.

Restraint, he argues, in response to the accusation that such a display of emotion was 'absurd', is something of which civilized men have little need. For them – each with his 'two good addresses' – the need for self-control is lessened by the existence of socially imposed constraints. You do not need to worry about the morality or advisability of eating the inhabitants of neighbouring villages if there is, in your own, a butcher able at all times to satisfy your demand for fresh meat. (We are reminded, by way of contrast, of Marlow's respect for the restraint of his cannibal crew in resisting – for whatever reason – the presumably powerful temptation to turn against their vastly outnumbered white employers.) Nor do you need to worry about exercising absolute control over your own aggressive instincts if there is a policeman constantly on hand to remind you of the advisability of keeping them in check. Those with 'solid pavement' under their feet, 'surrounded by kind neighbours ... stepping delicately between the butcher and the policeman, in the holy terror of scandal and gallows and lunatic asylums', cannot possibly understand the strains imposed on a person's self-control and 'innate strength' by the solitude and silence of the wilderness. Such strains may lead a man like Marlow to come close to tears in the uninhibited expression of his grief; they may lead a man like Kurtz to even worse excesses.

Though Marlow does little more than hint – either here or in later pages of *Heart of Darkness* – at what these excesses might be,[1] he clearly attributes them to the growth of a too great intimacy between Kurtz and the jungle, to something suggestive of atavistic reversion. The man has become a 'spoiled and pampered' child whom the wilderness has 'patted ... on the head'. The outward and visible sign of this favouritism has been his singular success in acquiring ivory for the Company:

Heaps of it, stacks of it. The old mud shanty was bursting with it. You would think there was not a single tusk left either above or below the ground in the whole country ... We filled the steamboat with it, and had to pile a lot on the deck. (pages 84–5)

Such is the closeness of his identification with his ivory that Marlow suggests that the hairless and 'lofty frontal bone of Mr Kurtz' has actually been turned into a ball of ivory by the Midas touch of his surroundings. This misleadingly playful image subtly aligns Marlow's reference to the sick and emaciated Kurtz as a 'disinterred body' with his later mention of the fact that most of the ivory on which this 'prodigy' has built his reputation is 'fossil', the natives having at some time attempted to conceal it from collectors by burying it in the ground.

Kurtz, we learn, is obsessed with his acquisitions and speaks as if the ivory – together with his fiancée back in Europe, the Inner Station, even the river itself – is his exclusive property. Such blind possessiveness, itself the moral counterpart of Kurtz's ultimate physical condition, stupefies Marlow to such an extent that he almost expects the wilderness to 'burst into a prodigious peal of laughter' at its impertinence. In the final analysis, however, what matters is not the trifling consideration of what Kurtz can or cannot in all honesty claim to own, so much as the realization that he has, in his turn, become the possession of some unimaginable dark force. The ostensibly loving caress of the wilderness has destroyed him both physically (he is 'withered', his flesh is 'consumed') and spiritually, his soul having been 'sealed ... to [the jungle's] own by the inconceivable ceremonies of some devilish initiation'. He has, in Marlow's cryptic phrase, 'literally' taken 'a high seat amongst the devils of the land', having presided 'at certain midnight dances ending with unspeakable rites, which ... were offered up to him'. Details of his final condition must at all costs be withheld from his Intended. Indeed, Marlow makes it plain that women have no place in a world where civilized humanity can undergo such a transformation:

They ... should be out of it. We must help them to stay in that beautiful world of their own, lest ours gets worse. (page 84)

By this time of Marlow's recounting of the story aboard the *Nellie*, however, Kurtz is dead; the 'initiated wraith from the back of Nowhere' has 'vanished altogether'. In attempting to account for the enormous transformation (the change from 'emissary of pity, and science, and progress' to initiate of the unspeakable) which he underwent during his last months, Marlow reveals a tension in Kurtz's origins and a paradox in his philosophy. In the first place, though his 'partly' English education had fostered in Kurtz sympathies and ideals similar to those on which British colonialism – a type of colonialism of which we know already, from his preamble, that Marlow approves – is founded, the continental aspect in his makeup was notably strong. In the context of the epidemic rapacity of the late nineteenth-century rush for Africa, the assertion that 'all Europe contributed to the making of Kurtz' has a ring that is more than a little sinister. Then there is the matter of the report that Kurtz undertook for the International Society for the Suppression of Savage Customs. Marlow recalls how he tingled with enthusiasm at the vibrant eloquence of its seventeen closely written pages, at its 'burning noble words' and magnificent peroration. But he also reflects on the ominous nature of its opening argument that 'we whites . . . "must necessarily appear to them [savages] in the nature of supernatural beings – we approach them with the might as of a deity"', he notes its complete lack of any practical suggestion as to how savage customs might indeed be suppressed, and he draws particular attention to its incongruous footnote, 'scrawled evidently much later, in an unsteady hand . . . "Exterminate all the brutes!"'

Marlow concludes this digressive glance forward at the character of Kurtz by returning to the theme of restraint and comparing Kurtz's lack of this much prized quality with that displayed by the 'poor fool' of a helmsman. Restraint, we recall, is an attribute that Marlow freely admires in his native crew; it is not one that he associates with the pilgrims, who respond to periodic emergencies both ashore and on board the steamboat with a good deal of unproductive arm-waving and lead-squirting. At the crucial moment of the attack, however, the helmsman's natural instinct deserts him, with fatal consequences: he quits his post, reopens the pilot-house shutter that Marlow was at such pains to close a few moments earlier, and partakes in the hysteria of the whites by opening up with the Martini-Henry: 'He had no restraint, no restraint – just like Kurtz – a tree swayed by the wind' (page 88). Kurtz's moral demise is a direct result of his removal from the constraining influence of western society and of his failure to cultivate any compensatory self-restraint. Like the helmsman, he responds to the pressures of circumstance by abandoning the standards and morality appropriate to his upbringing and embracing those of another – and alien – culture.

We are, perhaps, invited to wonder at this juncture what might happen to Marlow were he to be exposed to the conditions that have brought about Kurtz's downfall. The two men, after all, have a number of characteristics in common: English idealism tainted with continental opportunism (Marlow, we recall, did not hesitate to ask his aunt to use her influence with the Company's administration in order to secure a position for him), the reputation (whether deserved or not) of being exceptionally gifted, and a susceptibility to the call of the wilderness.

23. Arrival at the Inner Station (*pages 88–92*)

The second part of *Heart of Darkness* concludes with a description of the steamboat's arrival at the Inner Station. After his somewhat piecemeal and nebulous attempt 'to account to [himself] for the shade of Mr Kurtz', Marlow now resumes a more careful chronology and turns his attention once again to themes introduced and in part developed before his digression.

He begins by relating the circumstances of the dead helmsman's 'simple funeral'. This is the man, we should remember, for whom Marlow has already expressed his contempt in crypto-racist terms:

He sported a pair of brass earrings, wore a blue cloth wrapper from the waist to the ankles, and thought all the world of himself. He was the most unstable kind of fool I had ever seen. He steered with no end of a swagger while you were by; but if he lost sight of you, he became instantly the prey of an abject funk, and would let that cripple of a steamboat get the upper hand of him in a minute. (page 79)

In spite of these shortcomings and the fact of the helmsman's erratic behaviour when the vessel came under fire from the shore, however, Marlow now insists that he misses him 'awfully', sensing in his death not only the breaking of a bond of dependency but also that of a partnership. His admission that he has only come to recognize the true nature of these ties at the moment of their destruction is reminiscent of the way in which his fixation with Kurtz becomes most intense when he believes hopes for his survival to be utterly futile. But the bond that unites Marlow with the dead native goes a good deal deeper than the purely professional: 'the intimate profundity of that look he gave me when he received his hurt', he tells his listeners, 'remains to this day in my memory – like a claim of distant kinship affirmed in a supreme moment'. This feeling of shared humanity with someone so markedly different from and – it would appear – inferior to himself recalls Marlow's comments on the natives who paddled their canoes through the surf to visit his ship during the voyage out, the unaccountable stirrings he experienced at the sound of drums and dancing ashore as he piloted his own shabby steamboat up the river, and his admiration for the calm under pressure and the inexplicable restraint displayed by his cannibal crew.

On this particular occasion, Marlow's feelings of kinship prompt him to tip the helmsman's body overboard as expeditiously as possible. What appears to the congregation of pilgrims on the awning-deck as 'heartless promptitude' (their chattering is, with an appropriate shift of imagery, likened to that of a flock of magpies, birds noted both for their raucousness and their thievery) and to the survivors among '[his] friends, the wood-cutters' as unreasonable waste, is in fact an act of loving farewell. He cannot – he tells his listeners – bear to look at what he is doing as he jerks the spear out of the dead man's side; he hugs the body 'desperately' from behind, supporting it in such a way that the shoulders are pressed to his breast; he watches as the current snatches it like 'a wisp of grass', keeping his gaze on it until it disappears for ever from his view. As if embarrassed by the depth of his feelings, however, he characteristically, and not entirely convincingly, proposes other motives for the speediness of his action: namely his desire to avoid 'startling trouble' between passengers and crew, and his anxiety to ensure the safety of his command by taking over the wheel himself.

The brutal but essentially unproductive nature of white colonial enterprise is another theme to which Marlow returns in these pages. Represented earlier in his narrative by the French man-of-war pointlessly shelling the African coastline and by the 'objectless blasting' entailed in the construction of the railway at the Company Station, it is here exemplified by the fusillade with which the pilgrims respond to the attack launched on them from the shore. At all three moments, Marlow focuses on the contrast between design and achievement. The ship's grand intention of 'war' on its hidden 'enemies' is expressed in lilliputian gestures: 'Pop ... a small flame ... a little white smoke ... a tiny projectile ... a feeble screech.' The 'heavy and dull detonation' from the excavations at the Company Station likewise produces nothing more than 'a puff of smoke'. The pilgrims' present action of 'simply squirting lead into [the] bush' in answer to the hail of arrows has, as Marlow is at pains to show, an equally farcical aspect:

I had seen, from the way the tops of the bushes rustled and flew, that almost all the shots had gone too high. You can't hit anything unless you take aim and fire from the shoulder; but these chaps fired from the hip with their eyes shut. (page 89)

However, in this case, the 'deuce of a lot of smoke' produced by the action also spells potential disaster, since it hinders the safe navigation of the steamboat through a particularly difficult channel. By developing, in this way, one of the novella's recurrent themes, Marlow is able to demonstrate his conviction that colonial enterprise, for all its seemingly harmless absurdity, in fact possesses the capacity to interfere (perhaps fatally) with real and solid values – values of which, as we have seen, he regards the boat to be the actual physical embodiment. Significantly, it is not the pilgrims' fire-power that scares off the attackers, but the screeching of the vessel's steam-whistle.

Marlow has already devoted some time to establishing the notorious unreliability of first impressions and of judgements made on the basis of imported perceptions, using as illustrations (among other things) the sandbank, the attack and its consequences, and the question of Kurtz's survival. He now returns to this theme and candidly reveals the inaccuracy of conclusions he drew at the time of the steamboat's brief fuelling stop, fifty miles downstream, at the abandoned settlement where he found the freshly stitched copy of Towson's *Inquiry*. On that occasion, the book and the warning message on the wood-pile led him to the belief that the place's previous occupant was an Englishman like himself, while the fact that he was unable to make head or tail of the notes pencilled in the margin of the book suggested their being written in some sort of cipher. The wrongness of these assumptions is made clear when, on the arrival of the steamboat off the Inner Station, we are introduced to a 'white man under a hat like a cartwheel' who stands 'beckoning persistently' to the newcomers from the shore, and who is soon revealed as author of both message and notes. He is, however, not English but Russian, 'son of an arch-priest . . . Government of Tambov', and the pencillings in his copy of Towson – whose restoration he greets with ecstasy – are not in cipher but in Cyrillic script.

This recovery of perspective – with the incidental clearing up of what, at the time, seemed to Marlow 'an extravagant mystery' – takes place aboard the steamboat. From his battle-scarred pilot-house, Marlow is able to make out some of the details of the Inner Station itself. Its general appearance is similar to that of other settlements he has visited: the long building on the summit of the hill is 'decaying . . . half buried in the high grass', there are gaping holes in its roof, and whatever formerly existed in the way of protective enclosure or fence has all but disappeared, leaving 'half-a-dozen slim posts . . . in a row, roughly trimmed, and with their upper ends ornamented with round carved balls' (page 89). Despite the fact that, by his own admission, Marlow notes all this detail 'from afar' (the boat has not yet, for reasons of safety, come inshore and his observations are made with the aid of his binoculars), he presents it with remarkable certainty, apparently – and ironically – ignoring the various lessons that his experiences have taught him about the deceptiveness of appearances.

Interestingly, it is the Russian, with his harlequin appearance and boyish enthusiasm, that engages Marlow's attention on arrival at the station. Though, as he manoeuvres his boat inshore, his first concern is for Kurtz, he does not join the armed party of pilgrims that sets off immediately for the decaying house on the hill. Instead, mindful of the likelihood that a quick getaway will be called for, he remains at his post aboard the steamboat and occupies the interim entertaining the strangely-dressed young man, of whom it quickly becomes clear that he approves. To begin with, the Russian is a fellow-sailor and possesses a sailor's foresight and practicality, the one evidenced by his arrangement of the wood-pile complete with its warning message, the other by his careful restitching of Towson's *Inquiry* and the beautifully executed patchwork of his attire. As he draws Marlow's attention to yet another snag lying in the vessel's path, we realize that, throughout the journey upriver, it has fallen to Marlow, and him alone, to watch for and negotiate such dangers. The two men, furthermore, share an admiration for Towson's 'honest concern for the right way of going to work' as well as the conviction that 'one good screech' from the steamboat's whistle will do more to scare off an attack from the native population than any amount of random rifle-firing. Above all – continuing a theme introduced in Marlow's preamble, in the account of his visit to the 'sepulchral city' and in his digression on Kurtz's origins – 'the harlequin' meets with approval because of the strength of his English connections: his command of the language is fluent; he inquires, 'all smiles', as to whether Marlow is English and exhibits regret at not being able to claim as much for himself; he eulogizes English tobacco and reveals that he spent part of his sea-going apprenticeship 'in the English ships'. All of which sets him a good way apart from the incompetent and rascally pilgrims. Indeed, it is fitting that such should turn out to be the character and background of a man who – if the remarks Marlow overheard the Manager making to his uncle at the Central Station are to be credited – has for some time been a thorn in the flesh of the Company administration.

Marlow's account of his new acquaintance centres principally on the harlequin's youthful innocence. He has a 'beardless, boyish face, very fair' and largely unfeatured, his 'open countenance' registering his frequent emotional changes with smiles and frowns that '[chase] each other . . . like sunshine and shadow on a wind-swept plain'. His narrative, especially when it focuses on himself, is a released flood of excited gabble, often accompanied by expansive gesturing, and Marlow admits to finding it more than a little overwhelming. Only when he thinks of

Kurtz, or is reminded of his condition, is his vivacious flow interrupted by brief moments of seriousness or despondency. He is motivated by a youthful idealism and spirit of adventure, having embarked on his solo trading career out of a desire to 'see things, gather experience, ideas; enlarge the mind'. Having, through sheer persistence, persuaded a Dutch trading-house to fit him out, he has come to the interior with – and in this he is not unlike the pilgrims Marlow has encountered – 'a light heart, and no more idea of what would happen to him than a baby'. What has happened to him, in fact, is that he has met and – like the natives who 'don't want him to go' – fallen under the spell of Kurtz. Like others before him, he has come to regard this 'gifted creature' as a kind of guru, to whom he listens with deep absorption but with whom he does not consider himself worthy of conversation. (We are reminded of Marlow's own growing conviction that his meeting with Kurtz will be an auditory rather than a physical experience.) The second part of *Heart of Darkness* comes to its striking conclusion with a picture of the harlequin – his arms extended wide, his 'little blue . . . perfectly round' eyes staring at Marlow – declaring that the chief of the Inner Station has enlarged his mind. The irony of this picture lies, of course, in its strategic positioning so soon after Marlow's disclosure of the lack of restraint that has led to Kurtz's taking 'a high seat amongst the devils of the land'.

Part Three

24. Conversation with the Harlequin (*pages 93–8*)

If, to Marlow's way of thinking, the – as yet – unseen Kurtz represents both 'the most exalted' and 'the most contemptible' power of words, the harlequin is the embodiment of an equally enigmatic 'insoluble problem'. As the two men converse, Marlow is 'lost in astonishment' not merely at the Russian's extraordinary appearance, manner and devotion to Kurtz, but at 'his very existence', which seems 'improbable, inexplicable, and altogether bewildering', considering 'his destitution, his loneliness, the essential desolation of his futile wanderings'. Marlow attributes his survival to an 'unpractical spirit of adventure' and to the fact that his life is not governed by the cowardly and calculating attitudes of his fellow-whites:

there he was gallantly, thoughtlessly alive, to all appearance indestructible solely by the virtue of his few years and of his unreflecting audacity. (page 93)

He finds himself close to envying 'this be-patched youth' the 'modest and clear flame' that burns within him. He does not, however, envy his devotion to Kurtz, a devotion over which he has not, it would seem, reflected sufficiently deeply, having accepted it 'with a sort of eager fatalism'. Beside the extreme moral dangers to which he has subjected himself by entering into this relationship, the physical perils the harlequin has braved in the course of his ever deeper penetration into the continent's dark interior have been mere trifles. He has, however, been blinded to such dangers by the power of Kurtz's conversation to make him 'see things', and by the fascination of a personality that has entirely 'filled his life, occupied his thoughts, swayed his emotions'.

For all his admiration of the man, however, the harlequin acknowledges that there is also a 'terrible' side to Kurtz, one manifest chiefly in the latter's moody unpredictability and lack of restraint and in his readiness to employ force in the achievement of his objectives – characteristics up to this point in the narrative associated firmly in the mind of the reader with trigger-happy pilgrims rather than with emissaries of 'pity, and science, and progress'. The young Russian has often witnessed the effect of this potentially lethal combination on the native population and discloses that it is now the principal means by which Kurtz obtains his ivory. On this issue, he can, indeed, speak from personal experience:

> I had a small lot of ivory the chief of that village near my house gave me . . . Well, he wanted it, and wouldn't hear reason. He declared he would shoot me unless I gave him the ivory and then cleared out of the country, because he could do so, and had a fancy for it, and there was nothing on earth to prevent him killing whom he jolly well pleased. And it was true, too. I gave him the ivory . . . But I didn't clear out. No, no. I couldn't leave him. (page 95)

His toleration of such treatment is explained by his conviction that Kurtz is different from ordinary men and that, as such, he deserves to be judged differently. He has 'suffered too much', being torn between a profound and deepening hatred for his circumstances and way of life, and a fascination which makes it impossible for him to break away from them. Rationalization of this sort does not, of course, lessen the physical dangers to which the harlequin exposes himself by staying at the Inner Station. Marlow notes the pride with which he mentions that he has 'managed to nurse Kurtz through two illnesses' and the fact that he alludes to his achievement 'as you would to some risky feat'. He also comes to the conclusion that Kurtz, with his uncharacteristically violent and unpredictable behaviour and his prolonged excursions into the jungle to 'forget himself amongst [the] people', has in fact gone mad.

As 'Kurtz's last disciple' continues his 'amazing tale' aboard the steamboat, Marlow remarks the intense stillness of the surrounding woods, a stillness which suggests their possession of some secret knowledge which intruders like himself cannot share, and their unassailable patience in awaiting the inevitable termination of the intrusion. The contrast he draws between the young sailor's excitable and disjointed narrative manner, with its 'desolate exclamations . . . shrugs . . . interrupted phrases . . . hints ending in deep sighs', and the vast impassivity of the natural background, reminds us of a similar contrast in Marlow's account of the conversation between the Manager and his uncle at the Central Station. On the present occasion, the impression is particularly striking:

> I looked around, and I don't know why, but I assure you that never, never before, did this land, this river, this jungle, the very arch of this blazing sky, appear to me so hopeless and so dark, so impenetrable to human thought, so pitiless to human weakness. (page 94)

His consciousness that the silent stillness of the hillside on which Kurtz's dilapidated house is located may conceal equally silent watchers makes Marlow uneasy, and, in an effort to settle his mind one way or the other, he takes up his binoculars once again and proceeds to examine the terrain at closer quarters. Ironically, it is not his fears about the natives so much as his fears about Kurtz that are confirmed by what he sees.

Marlow's binoculars provide him with the opportunity to develop further those descriptive techniques, based on the workings of pictorial impressionism, which he employed earlier in *Heart of Darkness* in his accounts of the river shoals below the Inner Station and the attack from the shore. With the former he was, as we have seen, at pains to demonstrate how the unclear, perhaps even misleading, effect produced by a distant object on the eye of an observer may be gradually focused into sharp fact as the space between object and observer is closed: 'an islet' becomes 'a mere grassy hummock of bright green' becomes 'the head of a long sandbank', while the 'sandbank' itself becomes 'a chain of shallow patches' which is eventually seen to bear the likeness of 'a man's backbone ... under the skin'. With the latter, it is not the abbreviation of physical space that allows actuality to emerge from Marlow's initial, erroneous impressions; it is the passage of that minute fraction of time – artificially extended by the operation of the narrative – which is required for the completion of the deductive process. In other words, Marlow's understanding of the true nature of the 'little sticks' and the helmsman's clumsiness is the result of the closing of a mental rather than a spatial gap.

With the aid of his binoculars, Marlow now plays a further variation on this theme of emergent reality. From his vantage-point on the steamboat he surveys the hillside, 'sweeping the limit of the forest at each side and at the back of the house'. There is no sign of life. The only difference between what he now observes and the impression of the place he received while the boat was hovering cautiously off-shore is one of scale: things that were previously seen 'from afar' – Kurtz's house with its ruined roof and long mud wall 'peeping above the grass' – now seem to be close enough to touch. A sudden sharp movement brings into his field of vision one of the half dozen ornamented posts that distance previously suggested to be all that remained of the building's protective fence. His reaction to what he sees is remarkable:

Now I had suddenly a nearer view, and its first result was to make me throw my head back as if before a blow. (page 96)

Its remarkableness lies in its demonstration of how violently physical an effect an object that in reality lies beyond the range of his natural vision – one, indeed, whose existence he is in no immediate position to verify – can have on the very observer who, mere hours earlier, responded to arrows clattering all around him and men falling dead at his feet, first with incomprehension, then with sang-froid. Having regained his composure, Marlow proceeds to examine the neighbouring poles and realizes his error in previously identifying as carved ornamentation what are, in fact, 'heads on . . . stakes'. At the same time as confessing one mistake he appears to stumble into another, offering as he does – without further consideration – the opinion that the heads 'would have been even more impressive . . . if their faces had not been turned to the house'. In offering this opinion, he implies a belief that the purpose of the macabre display is entirely practical: the deterrence of intruders and the striking of fear into potential dissenters. A few lines later, however, he tells his listeners that there is 'nothing exactly profitable in these heads being there' and makes it clear that he sees them as being in some way connected with the 'gratification of [Kurtz's] various lusts'. Of the six heads, the only one that is turned in his direction is that of which he first caught an accidental glimpse through his binoculars. In his deliberate description of the gruesome object, he once again draws our attention to the close (and sometimes ironical) relationship between the real and the apparent, between what actually is and what it seems to be:

[T]here it was, black, dried, sunken, with closed eyelids – a head that seemed to sleep at the top of that pole, and, with the shrunken dry lips showing a narrow white line of teeth, was smiling, too, smiling continuously at some endless and jocose dream of that eternal slumber. (page 97)

Of course, the fantastic effects Marlow describes have existence for him only through the agency of his binoculars. They lack the solid substance of the steamboat beneath his feet or the immediacy of his conversation with the young Russian. For this reason, the jolt they gave him – occasioned, so he maintains, by surprise rather than shock – is temporary and superficial. When he puts his glasses down, it is as if 'the head that had appeared near enough to be spoken to' is sent leaping, out of the reality of his present existence, back 'into inaccessible distance'.

The sight of the impaled heads, indeed, gives Marlow significantly less trouble than does the thought of Kurtz's willing participation in various unnamed and unnamable native rituals, details of which he peremptorily prevents the harlequin from recounting. 'Pure, uncomplicated savagery' is, in his estimation, 'a positive relief' compared to such 'subtle horrors'. He falls to considering how a 'special being', a very prodigy on whom the Company has pinned so many of its hopes, the one person who (in Marlow's own words) 'had come out here with moral ideas of some sort', could have undergone such a change. Recent revelations and discoveries suggest that Kurtz is and, in fact, always has been 'hollow at the core', that there is an essential deficiency in his make-up which his 'magnificent eloquence' may serve briefly to disguise, but for which it cannot in the long term compensate. Kurtz has, in other words, no more real moral or spiritual substance than the Chief Accountant of the Company Station, whom Marlow referred to earlier as having the appearance of 'a hairdresser's dummy', or the 'papier-mâché Mephistopheles' of a brickmaker. The wilderness into which he has intruded has 'found him out' – just as it has found out and exposed the Accountant's mania for efficiency and his concomitant indifference to the lot of others, and the aristocratic brickmaker's envious and crudely pursued ambitions – and it has taken 'a terrible vengeance for the fantastic invasion'. (Significantly, 'fantastic invasion' is precisely the phrase used of the General Manager and his buccaneering uncle in Marlow's account of the evening stroll the two men take along the riverbank at the Central Station. This same Manager, moreover, who owes his position of authority purely to the accident of his immunity to disease, believes that all those who 'come out' as Company agents should, like him, 'have no entrails.') Kurtz's spiritual void has made him an easy prey to his wild surroundings, which have – with an irresistible fascination – 'whispered to him things about himself which he did not know, things of which he had no conception till he took counsel with this great solitude' (page 97). Paradoxically, his insatiable appetite for ivory, ascendancy over the natives and unrestrained indulgence of his 'various lusts' have in no way diminished the flow of Kurtz's 'splendid monologues on . . . love, justice, conduct of life'. Unlike Marlow, the harlequin appears to detect little incongruity in this, and makes the point that the impaled heads are those of 'rebels'. His doing so immediately aligns Kurtz's attitudes and actions, in the mind of the reader, with those of the officers aboard the French man-of-war shelling their invisible 'enemies' in the bush, and with those of the Company agents who excuse the shackling, abuse and slaughter of their native employees by referring to them as 'criminals'. As if to underline the irony that he sees in all this, Marlow bursts out laughing.

25. Enter Kurtz (*pages 98–104*)

Marlow's conversation with the harlequin is interrupted by the un-expected appearance, round a corner of the station-house, of the pil-grims, walking 'in a compact body' and 'bearing an improvised stret-cher in their midst'. Their progress down the hillside towards the stea-mer is halted by an outpouring from 'the darkfaced and pensive forest' of streams of armed and potentially aggressive natives. Marlow watches through his binoculars as Kurtz – the man on the stretcher – raises himself in order to address this 'crowd of men made of dark and glittering bronze'. What he sees is a figure (remarkably reminiscent of the inhabitants of the grove of death at the Company's Station) so wasted that it seems rather some 'atrocious phantom ... apparition ... animated image of death carved out of old ivory ... shadow' than a living being. Its flesh has retreated so far that, from a distance, little more than an extended outline of bones – skull, rib-cage, arm – is apparent, emerging from its displaced covering 'as from a winding-sheet'. (Was Marlow's perception of the shoals that guard the river approach to the Inner Station as 'a man's backbone ... running down the middle of his back under the skin' an unconscious prediction of what he was to find on his arrival?) For all its shrivelled aspect, how-ever, the figure of Kurtz seems 'at least seven feet long', and Marlow comments on the irony that provides a man so built with a name suggestive of shortness. Nor is this the only contradiction he notes about the ailing station chief. For all his emaciation, when Kurtz opens his mouth to speak, he assumes a 'weirdly voracious aspect', as if about to swallow everything – air, earth, men – that lies before him. (This portrait perhaps owes something to that of Death, who, in Book Two of Milton's *Paradise Lost*, is depicted as a black 'shadow', greedy to consume everything that crosses his path.) When Kurtz's bearers once again take up the stretcher, Marlow notes that they stagger under its unexpected weight. Interest-ingly, this is precisely how he too reacts when, on a subsequent occasion, he offers Kurtz physical assistance. The detail he includes in the account of this later incident suggests that he sees it as a grotesque parody of the St Christopher story, in which a strong giant finds himself unable to support the weight of a small child whom he has agreed to carry across a river, only to discover that the child is in fact

Christ and that in his body he carries the weighty cares of the whole world:

I wiped my forehead, while my legs shook under me as though I had carried half a ton on my back down that hill. And yet I had only supported him, his bony arm clasped round my neck – and he was not much heavier than a child. (page 108)

A third contradiction is made plain when Marlow finally comes to hear for himself the voice of this man who appears to be so exhausted that he '[does] not seem capable of a whisper'. He is amazed at 'the volume of tone' Kurtz produces, apparently without effort and with only the slightest movement of his lips. 'A voice! a voice!' he acknowledges with some wonderment. 'It was grave, profound, vibrating.'

In spite of all Marlow has seen and heard of the man and his activities, both in the course of his voyage of enlightenment upriver and since his arrival at the Inner Station, his sympathies continue to be directed towards Kurtz rather than towards the Manager and his cronies. It is possible that he is encouraged in his attitude by Kurtz's brief gesture of recognition ('I am glad') at their first meeting. It is further possible that he is impressed with the directness and courage of the dying man's denunciation of the pilgrims. He certainly mentions both. However, it is the Manager's thinly-disguised exultation over Kurtz's plight, his wheedling attempts to get Marlow to concur with his condemnation of the agent's methods, and the vindictive glee with which he discloses his intention of referring all to 'the proper quarter' that affect Marlow most profoundly. It seems to him that the Manager's conversation has poisoned the very air and he '[turns] mentally to Kurtz for relief – positively for relief'. In spite of all that has been and can be said against Kurtz, he remains 'a remarkable man'. Marlow realizes immediately that the making of such an assertion must exclude him once and for all from the sphere of managerial favour.

Though he views this particular development with some relief, Marlow fully recognizes that any kind of allegiance to Kurtz is bound to have its nightmarish aspect. Nevertheless, when – a matter of moments later – the harlequin hesitates to confide in him, as a brother seaman, 'knowledge of matters that would affect Mr Kurtz's reputation' he encourages the young man to speak openly, assuring him that he is indeed 'Mr Kurtz's friend – in a way'. No doubt it is the qualifying coda that Marlow adds to his guarantee that causes the harlequin to vacillate further. At all events, it is not until Marlow accepts personal responsibility for the safety of 'Mr Kurtz's reputation' that he reveals that the attack on the steamer was ordered by Kurtz himself, and that its

BUT NOT FOR MORAL REASO[N]

purpose was to scare the pilgrims into abandoning their quest, thus allowing him to remain indefinitely in his own place, among his own people. Even after he has passed on this dangerous piece of information, the Russian continues to display apprehension over the possibility of its being circulated in the wrong quarters. Only when Marlow 'promise[s] a complete discretion with great gravity' (and, in so doing, demonstrates for a second time his willingness to bend the truth) does he at last appear to be satisfied. His fearful obsession with what the world might think of Kurtz if the extent of and motives for his attempted manipulation of events were to come to light is plainly rooted in his idolization of the madman who has 'enlarged [his] mind'. Marlow's incredulity at such blind and misplaced devotion leads him to the observation – as the young man finally vanishes into the night – that, in retrospect, he finds it difficult to believe that such a 'phenomenon' ever really existed.

Some further understanding of the means by which the wilderness exercises its power over Kurtz is provided by Marlow's account of what happens on the shore once the agent has been brought safely aboard the steamer. Three figures appear, as if from nowhere. The sole function of two of these – 'bronze . . . leaning on tall spears . . . under fantastic head-dresses of spotted skins, warlike and still' – seems to be to accompany and support the third. Marlow's description gives them something of the air of funerary statues at an ancient burial and, in that respect, associates them in the reader's mind with the two women who '[guard] the door of Darkness' at the Company's headquarters in the sepulchral city. The third figure, moving 'from right to left along the lighted shore', is that of a wild- and gorgeous-seeming woman, whom Marlow senses to be a projection or embodiment of 'the immense wilderness' itself –

in the hush that had fallen suddenly upon the whole sorrowful land . . . the colossal body of the fecund and mysterious life seemed to look at her, pensive, as though it had been looking at the image of its own tenebrous and passionate soul (page 101)

– and whose appearance and actions he accordingly describes in careful detail. What he shows us is a compound of contradictions in which the splendidly martial (her hair in the shape of a helmet, her leggings and gauntlets made of brass wire, presumably supplied – like the 'pay' for Marlow's cannibal crew – from Company sources) is set beside the cheap and trivial ('innumerable necklaces of glass beads . . . bizarre things, charms, gifts of witch-men'). Though she walks confidently, 'with measured steps . . . treading the earth proudly', the glittering abundance of her ornaments makes her appear to '[tremble] at every step'. She is at once 'superb . . . magnificent . . . stately' and 'savage . . . wild-eyed . . . ominous'. Her look, as she gazes towards the steamer where Kurtz lies, is a mixture of tragedy and ferocity, of fear and resolve. As she comes abreast of the vessel, she stops and directly faces the men watching her from its decks. As if anxious lest his listeners should miss the significance of the connection he has already proposed, Marlow likens her a second time to the wilderness, immobile and 'with an air of brooding over an inscrutable purpose'. What that purpose might be is made clear by the woman's ritual movement of opening her bared arms and throwing them above her head, in such a way that the shadows so formed '[sweep] around the river, gathering the steamer into a shadowy embrace'. It is worth recalling that when, shortly after his arrival at the Inner Station, Marlow asked the harlequin for an explanation of the attack on the steamer, he was furnished with the reply that 'they don't want him to go'. The woman's gesture is symbolic confirmation of this reply which, under the present circumstances, takes on a new and wider significance. When the harlequin originally made the remark, 'they' appeared to refer simply to the attackers or (at most) the tribe in general; now, we discover that it includes – in the proud but sorrowing person of this striking woman – nothing less than the wilderness itself. In the light of the harlequin's disclosure as to who ordered the attack, moreover, it must also be taken to refer to the chief of the Inner Station himself.

In this way, the process by which Marlow comes to understand fully the implications of the words that he hears is seen to be directly parallel to that by which he comes to understand the significance of the various objects – shoals, arrows, impaled heads – that he sees. Words, like visual images, frequently convey general and perhaps misleading effects before they communicate clear facts.

There is a possible further significance in the figure of the woman. Some commentators[1] draw attention to the curious detail of the rigidity of her raised arms and suggest that the shadow she makes must in consequence be not so much one of embrace as of destruction, the boat and its occupants being fatally caught in a giant forfex. Is she to be identified, then, with Atropos, the third of the Fates of classical mythology, responsible for cutting with her shears the thread of human destiny? Does the black woman on the wilderness shore make a trio with the two black-clad knitters encountered by Marlow (as by all other aspiring agents) at the Company's European headquarters? Is she responsible, as such, for presiding over the termination of existences that have been shaped and woven by her sisterly counterparts? Certainly her appearance is enough seriously to unnerve the 'man of patches'. He contemplates shooting her if she so much as attempts to board the vessel, and assures Marlow that he has 'been risking [his] life every day for the last fortnight in order to keep her out of [Kurtz's] house'. Significantly, within a few days of her appearance on the shore, Kurtz will be dead.

26. Marlow's Mission Ashore (*pages 104–108*)

Marlow's promise to take on the responsibility of defending Kurtz's reputation is soon put to the test. Waking shortly after midnight, he notices a 'big fire' burning on the hillside and, 'deep within the forest, red gleams' marking the spot where 'Mr Kurtz's adorers [are] keeping their uneasy vigil'. The accompanying sounds of a monotonously beating drum and the drone-like chanting of many men act like a drug on his 'half-awake senses', and, as he leans over the boat's rail, he dozes off. He is brought to himself by a burst of yells from the shore and realizes almost immediately that Kurtz is no longer in the cabin in which his rescuers had placed him after carrying him – wasted and exhausted – down from his house. Ironically for someone who has so consistently been misled by appearances in the course of his recent adventures, Marlow does not at first believe his eyes. This incredulity fortuitously prevents his raising the alarm and enables him to keep his word to the departed harlequin:

I did not betray Mr Kurtz – it was ordered I should never betray him – it was written I should be loyal to the nightmare of my choice. (page 105)

Marlow associates his disbelief on this occasion with a 'sheer blank fright, pure abstract terror', which seems utterly unconnected with any impending physical danger to himself, being related rather to the appalling likelihood that Kurtz has succumbed once again to the lure of the wilderness and its unnamable rituals. Just as he earlier found the 'pure, uncomplicated savagery' of the impaled heads more acceptable than the prospect of the harlequin detailing the ceremonies customarily observed by the native chiefs in approaching Kurtz ('they would crawl'), so now Marlow comments that 'the usual sense of commonplace, deadly danger, the possibility of a sudden onslaught and massacre' seems positively welcome when set beside the 'moral shock' and the implications ('altogether monstrous, intolerable to thought and odious to the soul') of Kurtz's disappearance from his cabin. It is significant that the circumstances under which Kurtz demonstrates this particular lack of restraint, leaving the security of the steamer in order to answer the summons of the drums, duplicate those under which Marlow experienced a notable testing of his own powers of self-control on the journey upriver.

Marlow's mood changes radically once he has himself slipped ashore. Immediately, he finds himself exulting in the thrill of the chase – now striding purposefully through the wet grass with clenched fists, intent on catching up with his prey and 'giving him a drubbing'; now running in a wide semicircle in an effort to outflank Kurtz, and chuckling with satisfaction as if his manoeuvre were part of some childish recreation. Even the 'imbecile thought' of his being lost or cut off, of his never getting back to the steamer but living out his days alone and unarmed in the forest, adds spice to the adventure. Significantly, he confuses the beating of the drums with that of his own heart and notes his pleasure at its 'calm regularity'. His exhilaration is, however, short-lived. It does not take him long to realize that he has once again been the victim of an illusion, an illusion that – on this occasion – has been self-suggested. What, for a while, seemed little more than 'a boyish game' is in reality an extreme danger. Only when he confronts Kurtz some thirty yards from the nearest native fire and simultaneously observes the figure with 'antelope horns . . . on its head' silhouetted against its glow does he see the situation 'in its right proportion' and come fully to his senses.

Part of Marlow's initial enjoyment of the game of pursuit lies in his certainty of its successful outcome. He supposes that Kurtz, in his sick and fatigued state, is unable to walk, that he is in all probability 'crawling on all-fours' – an image which directly reminds us both of the dying native crawling to the river for water at the Company's Station and also of the ceremonial subservience of the native chiefs in their approach to Kurtz. Marlow's supposition suggests that the roles of dominator and dominated, of god and votarist – established in the 'inconceivable' rituals of access – have now been critically reversed. Kurtz, who once appeared to his people 'in the nature of [a] supernatural [being]', now demonstrates a grovelling and sinister dependence on them. The image has, moreover, a further powerful suggestion: as Ian Watt suggests, 'atavistic regression could hardly go further; a man crawling like an animal to be worshipped by followers in the ceremonial guise of animals'.[1] In this crucial moment, Marlow realizes that to him, and him alone, has fallen the burden of saving Kurtz's soul.

At first, he believes that it will require physical force to get Kurtz back to the sanctuary of the steamboat, but realization that any kind of struggle is certain to attract the attention of the figures round the fire causes him to drop the idea. By way of alternative, he tries persuasion – first questioning whether Kurtz really knows what he is doing, then suggesting that if he yields to the spell of the wilderness he will inevitably 'be lost . . . utterly lost'. Latching on to Kurtz's complaint that the arrival of the Manager ('this stupid scoundrel') has in any case effectively thwarted his 'immense plans' for the future of his station, Marlow urges him not to sacrifice – by giving in to 'gratified and monstrous passions' – the success he has achieved, the reputation of enlightenment that he has won among the administrators of the Company in Europe. It is an argument which Marlow himself knows to be dubious, if the self-conscious steadiness with which he advances it is anything to go by, but it happens to be one which Kurtz evidently finds irresistible. For though his is a soul that – lacking any kind of 'restraint . . . faith . . . fear' and 'struggling blindly with itself' – has gone mad, his intelligence remains perfectly clear. In his enforced self-sufficiency and elected isolation, he has learned how to '[kick] himself loose of the earth', so that moral imperatives inevitably give place in his mind to blatant self-interest. It is such self-interest that convinces him to accompany Marlow back to the boat.

27. The Death of Kurtz (*pages 108–13*)

In the course of his account of the steamer's journey downriver, Marlow takes up once again several important themes introduced, and in part developed, in the earlier stages of his narrative.

He returns, for one, to the powerfully active nature of the attraction exercised by the wilderness over the departing Kurtz. As the vessel swings out from the shore, the hillside and station clearing are filled with the 'naked, breathing, quivering, bronze bodies' of natives. They are led by bedaubed and antlered witch-men, intent on thwarting – by means of their shabby charms – the power that is forcibly removing a god from their midst. Predictably (we recall his tendency to see all blacks as stereotypically ignorant and superstitious), Marlow supposes that, to the natives, the steamboat must appear as a 'splashing, thumping, fierce river-demon beating the water with its terrible tail and breathing black smoke into the air'. The sorcerers seem to challenge one form of diabolism with another, uttering 'strings of amazing words that [resemble] no sounds of human language' and evoking from the crowd 'deep murmurs ... like the responses of some satanic litany'. The futility of their performance is made clear by the fact that, when Marlow – in an effort to disperse the crowd and thus prevent the gun-slinging pilgrims perpetrating a mindless and bloody massacre – repeatedly sounds the boat's steam-whistle, they fall face-down on the ground as if they have been shot dead.

Also present at the boat's departure, however, is the woman 'with helmeted head and tawny cheeks' whom, on her first appearance, Marlow described as seeming to be a physical projection of the 'tenebrous and passionate soul' of the wilderness. She cuts an altogether more impressive figure than the three sorcerers: when she stands at 'the very brink of the stream', puts out her hands and shouts in the direction of the steamer, for example, the crowd responds not with low, indistinct murmurs but with 'a roaring chorus of articulated, rapid, breathless utterance'. And when everyone else scatters in an effort to dodge 'the flying terror of the [whistle's] sound' she alone remains, motionless and unflinching, 'stretch[ing] tragically her bare arms ... over the sombre and glittering river'. Significantly, whereas the ceremonies of the witchmen excite no more response in Kurtz than an empty stare, the chorus of shouts whipped up by this 'barbarous and superb' woman produces a look of fiery longing in his eyes, and 'a mingled expression of wistfulness and hate'.

A second theme is that of moral and spiritual vacuity. Marlow has (as we have seen) taken the opportunity on more than one occasion to remark on the emptiness of men – like the Chief Accountant, the brickmaker and the General Manager – who bring no 'idea' to their participation in colonial enterprise. Even Kurtz, the one person who had apparently 'come out here with moral ideas of some sort', has – seduced by what the wilderness has to offer him – eventually been revealed as 'hollow at the core'. As he lies dying in the pilot-house, he continues in his preoccupation with the ephemeral 'images of wealth and fame':

My Intended, my station, my career, my ideas – these were the subjects for the occasional utterances of elevated sentiments. The shade of the original Kurtz frequented the bedside of the hollow sham, whose fate it was to be buried presently in the mould of primeval earth. But both the diabolical love and the unearthly hate of the mysteries it had penetrated fought for the possession of that soul satiated with primitive emotions, avid of lying fame, of sham distinction, of all the appearances of success and power. (page 110)

In the final analysis, there seems to be little to choose between Kurtz and the pilgrims, those 'mean and greedy phantoms' whose attitudes and activities Marlow has consistently deplored since his arrival in the Company's territory. It is, indeed, worth recalling that Marlow's first glimpse of Kurtz (being carried down the hillside at the Inner Station on a stretcher) reminded him of some 'atrocious phantom . . . apparition . . . animated image of death carved out of old ivory . . . shadow'. Moreover, he maintains the striking metaphor of Kurtz's 'ivory face' to the end.

T. S. Eliot was clearly aware of the applicability to his own times of the moral and spiritual emptiness Conrad portrays in *Heart of Darkness*: his taking as the motto for his poem 'The Hollow Men' (1925) the Manager's native servant's casual announcement that 'Mistah Kurtz – he dead' is both suggestive and celebrated.

Time and again, in the course of the novella, we have been reminded of Kurtz's special gift, 'his ability to talk, his words'. As he journeys upriver, Marlow's general interest in meeting the 'prodigy' is refined, first into a wish to converse with him, and eventually into a desire – almost a passion – to hear him speak. When he encounters the harlequin, moreover, he is told: 'You don't talk with that man – you listen to him.' It is, however, not merely Kurtz's facility with words that impresses his hearers, but the very sonority of his voice. Marlow is amazed, at their first encounter, that a man as physically debilitated as he should be capable of producing so great a volume of tone: 'A voice! a voice! It was grave, profound, vibrating.' As he draws towards the end of his story, Marlow becomes increasingly emphatic that Kurtz's 'gift of expression' – once the vehicle for his enlightened idealism – is now employed exclusively in the service of a contemptible lie:

Kurtz discoursed. A voice! a voice! It rang deep to the very last. It survived his strength to hide in the magnificent folds of eloquence the barren darkness of his heart. (page 110)

As elsewhere in *Heart of Darkness*, we are reminded of the danger of assuming that appearances necessarily provide a truthful reflection of actuality.

Significantly, as death approaches, both Kurtz's eloquence and his vocal resonance diminish. Marlow, on one of his regular visits to the pilot-house, finds him lying on his back with his eyes closed, muttering deliriously about the need to 'live rightly' before dying. Typically, the visitor erroneously assumes that what he hears is part of a speech Kurtz is rehearsing in his sleep, or perhaps 'a fragment of a phrase from some newspaper article'. He does not, apparently, understand it in the more immediate context of Kurtz's own confrontation with death. When, moreover, the dying man (significantly enveloped, as he is, in a physical darkness caused by the terminal failure of his sight) comes to the point of finally pronouncing what Marlow takes to be 'a judgement upon the adventures of his soul on this earth', he does so in an entirely uncharacteristic – though, under the circumstances, not inappropriate – tone of voice:

It was as though a veil had been rent . . . He cried in a whisper at some image, at some vision – he cried out twice, a cry that was no more than a breath – 'The horror! The horror!' (page 111)

Marlow speaks as someone who has himself peered into the abyss when he asserts to his listeners that the most a man can expect from life is some knowledge of himself. However, he suspects that such knowledge is afforded only those who actually make the 'last stride . . . over the edge'; that 'all the wisdom, and all truth, and all sincerity, are just compressed into that inappreciable moment of time in which we step over the threshold of the invisible'. At the moment of its utterance, Kurtz's last, whispered cry seems to be both an affirmation and a 'moral victory' – though it is a victory that has been dearly bought with the 'innumerable defeats . . . abominable terrors . . . abominable satisfactions' of his career. Marlow gives Kurtz credit for the fact that, having an unpalatable truth to own, he did not shrink from owning it; that – in his extreme moment – he did not hesitate to challenge, to deny the lie of his existence:

After all, this was the expression of some sort of belief; it had candour, it had conviction, it had a vibrating note of revolt in its whisper, it had the appalling face of a glimpsed truth. (page 113)

Kurtz's confrontation of the evil in his life takes place as the steamboat glides downstream, 'out of the heart of darkness'.

What, however, is the precise nature of the 'truth' that Kurtz glimpses in his final moments and how complete is his moral victory? Marlow is unclear, if not positively inconsistent, on both issues. In the first place, as Cedric Watts has pointed out,[1] what Marlow speaks of initially as an admission on Kurtz's part of the horrifying nature of his own past actions, he later presents as some kind of universal condemnation. He comments that, at the extreme moment, Kurtz's stare – a stare that condemns and loathes all that it encompasses – was 'wide enough to embrace the whole universe, piercing enough to penetrate all the hearts that beat in the darkness'. More problematical is Marlow's further hint that the victory implied by Kurtz's final words is only partial, that there coexists with his recognition of the horror a continuing absorption in it. The appallingness of the truth lies, in part at least, in its 'strange commingling of desire and hate'.

In the course of his account of Kurtz's final days, Marlow reminds his listeners of his conviction that practical concerns have been, for him, the only possible retreat from besetting fantasies and lies, that the honest work of getting his leaky command up the river and back again has on more than one occasion mercifully distracted him from both the mysterious appeal of the wilderness and the self-delusion and unrestrained self-seeking of his fellow-whites. Though he recognizes that, in some respects, he and Kurtz are cast in the same mould, he makes it clear that, when it comes to essentials, they are actually quite different: whereas his affiliation is with the honesty of work (we recall that, from the outset, the Company has thought of him as 'one of the Workers, with a capital') and with simple but direct action, the chief of the Inner Station stands for the high-sounding but deceitful word that proclaims one thing and performs another.

Marlow has, however, promised the harlequin that he will be responsible for Kurtz's reputation, and he has now compounded his responsibility by accepting custody of a certain 'packet of papers and a photograph – the lot tied together with a shoe-string': in doing so, he has – as he himself puts it – made choice of his own nightmare. As the boat slips downriver, he is forced to listen while the dying man talks (in 'contemptibly childish' fashion) of strategies for acceptance by the natives and advises him on the importance of a sound philosophical basis for action. He reflects on the paltriness of Kurtz's concerns by noting, once again, the vastness and timelessness of the setting; and he establishes his own resistance to them by focusing on the practical business of piloting his craft. When the steamer inevitably breaks down and is forced to lie up for repairs, Marlow prefers the unpalatable task of assisting the engineer and living 'in an infernal mess of rust, filings, nuts, bolts, spanners, hammers, ratchet-drills' to passing more of his time with his distinguished passenger.

28. Return to the Sepulchral City (*pages 113–16*)

There follows a lengthy gap in the otherwise careful chronology of Marlow's narrative – a gap occasioned by the severe and prolonged illness whose beginnings (in the form of attacks of the 'shakes') he traces to the period of the steamer's repair. He describes his struggle with death in the vaguest of terms: an 'unexciting contest' conducted 'in an impalpable greyness' and devoid of audience, emotion or conviction. He has been called to the threshold of the invisible but, unlike Kurtz, has 'been permitted to draw back [his] hesitating foot'. Indeed, if he has any knowledge at all of a man's last things, it is because he has been permitted to experience them vicariously through the extremity of Mr Kurtz.

Eventually he finds himself back in the 'sepulchral city' with various affairs to settle; but he is by no means yet fully recovered and 'totter[s] about the streets' with an abnormal temperature, in spite of his aunt's best efforts to 'nurse up [his] strength'. His attitude to the people of the city is distinctly hostile: like Gulliver newly returned from his voyage to the Houyhnhnms, he can find nothing to praise or respect. He contemplates the citizens 'hurrying through the streets to filch a little money from each other . . . to dream their insignificant and silly dreams' (page 113) with a resentment firmly based on the conviction that his experiences have endowed him with a knowledge of the world far superior to theirs. In retrospect, he acknowledges the inexcusability of such an attitude, putting it down to the acutely fevered state of his imagination at the time. Now, as he speaks to his audience aboard the *Nellie*, he is able to reflect rationally on all that has occurred. Being too close to an event – he implies – can result in as much interpretative distortion as being too far away from it. We are reminded, once again, of his earlier adventures with appearance and reality.

It is interesting to consider Marlow's various encounters on his return to Europe in the light of the precise structural symmetry that Conrad achieves in *Heart of Darkness*. The novella begins and ends with the primary narrator's description of the scene aboard the *Nellie*. Beneath this outer skin, as it were, lies the whole of Marlow's narrative, which – in its turn – begins (a brief transitional episode in London apart) and ends in the sepulchral city. Beneath this second skin lies the core of the work, Marlow's account of his African experiences. If we analyse this core, moreover, we discover that the symmetry continues deeper, with the up- and downriver journeys enclosing, at the psychological centre of the narrative, the steamer's arrival at the geographical 'heart of darkness'.

Given this overall pattern, it is worth noting that whereas, on his first visit to the sepulchral city, Marlow was one of many petitioners, on his second, he is very much the petitioned. Before setting out for Africa, he was entirely inexperienced and lacking in any but the most sketchy knowledge of what he was letting himself in for; he returns not only with these former deficiencies made good, but with an uncomfortable surplus of information on the subject of Kurtz. It is, indeed, not for himself but on account of his contact with Kurtz that he is obliged to receive a succession of visitors, each of whom displays a degree of oddity or perverseness. First to arrive is the clean-shaven Company official who comes seeking certain mysterious documents believed to be in Marlow's possession, but who leaves empty-handed after declining as inadequate Kurtz's eloquently worded report on the suppression of savage customs from which Marlow has taken the precaution of removing the damning final comment. Next is Kurtz's soi-disant cousin, anxious (for some undisclosed reason) 'to hear all the details about his dear relative's last moments', who eventually departs clutching 'some family letters and memoranda without importance'. Finally comes the journalist who passes judgement on the deficiency of his 'dear colleague['s] literary skills, but who is happy enough to carry off the 'famous Report' for publication.

After the last of these visitors has departed, all of Kurtz that Marlow is left with is a few letters and a portrait of his Intended. He feels the urge – though he cannot adequately explain it (does it spring from some sort of unconscious loyalty to the dead man? is it the working out of some deep-rooted human need?) – to disburden himself even of these:

All that had been Kurtz's had passed out of my hands: his soul, his body, his station, his plans, his ivory, his career. There remained only his memory and his Intended – and I wanted to give that up, too, to the past, in a way – to surrender personally all that remained of him with me . . . (page 116)

Accordingly, he decides to pay a visit to Kurtz's fiancée.

29. The Intended (*pages 116–21*)

Marlow's decision to make this visit is encouraged, to a great extent, by the image of the 'girl' that he receives from her portrait. Conscious, perhaps, of the many occasions upon which, in the course of his narrative, he has been obliged to admit to having been deceived by appearances, he qualifies his 'reading' of the picture by acknowledging that 'the sunlight can be made to lie, too'. He is convinced, none the less, that – in this instance – 'the delicate shade of truthfulness upon those features' is actual, not an illusion contrived by means of some 'manipulation of light and pose'. He senses that the person in the picture will be entirely receptive to all that he has to tell her:

She seemed ready to listen without mental reservation, without suspicion, without a thought for herself. (page 115)

His confidence in such matters is, however, characteristically misplaced.

To begin with, even the most cursory analysis of the pages of *Heart of Darkness* devoted to her interview with Marlow reveals that the Intended is more inclined to talk than to listen. She controls the direction of the conversation. She requires agreement on particular points. She puts words into her interlocutor's mouth, as when she takes for granted Marlow's admiration for her fiancé. In her enthusiasm, she completes one of Marlow's sentences in the most ludicrously inappropriate way:

'He was a remarkable man,' I said, unsteadily. Then before the appealing fixity of her gaze, that seemed to watch for more words on my lips, I went on. 'It was impossible not to –'
'Love him,' she finished eagerly. (page 118)

She talks 'as thirsty men drink', giving full rein to her self-deluding (and, at the same time, self-aggrandizing) adoration of Kurtz and his plans, his words, his example. She indulges in the opportunity that Marlow's presence affords for the unrestrained articulation of a grief that has, we understand, remained silent for over a year; and she does so in such a manner and to such a degree that her visitor is at last driven to request 'in a muffled voice' that she stop.

The preoccupation of this 'not very young' woman with mourning, with – in Lillian Feder's words – 'sacrific[ing] life to a dead ideal',[1] is given physical substance by Marlow's description of her surroundings.

Outside, the street in which she lives is 'still and decorous as a well-kept alley in a cemetery'. Inside, her drawing-room is lit by three long windows that have the appearance of 'luminous and bedraped columns', while its marble fireplace has 'a cold and monumental whiteness' and the grand piano that occupies one corner gleams darkly 'like a sombre and polished sarcophagus'. The darkness of the room – which grows steadily more palpable as the interview proceeds, so that, by its conclusion, Marlow is reduced to guessing the woman's actions from the sounds she makes – matches the misdirection of her attitude to Kurtz and obsession with preserving his memory.

The importance of the Intended to the thematic development of *Heart of Darkness* is reflected in the various parallels which exist between her and other of the novella's characters. Like the two concierges whom Marlow encountered at the Company offices at the outset of his adventures, for example, she is dressed entirely in black. She is also, like them, an anonymous and – particularly in the platitudinous nature of her grieving utterances – mechanical figure; like them, she is associated unequivocally with darkness and death. Moreover, within the overall symmetry of the narrative, her role as receiver (of the packet of letters, of Marlow himself and of such information about Kurtz as she will permit him to provide) carefully balances theirs as dispatchers.

There is more than a little, too, of Kurtz in his Intended. His culpable lack of restraint, for instance, has an obvious parallel in her uninhibited expression of grief, while his cadaverousness is matched – in the prevailing gloom of the drawing-room – by her wraith-like appearance:

She came forward, all in black, with a pale head, floating towards me in the dusk ... [her] fair hair ... pale visage ... pure brow, seemed surrounded by an ashy halo from which the dark eyes looked out at me. (page 117)

She is a 'tragic and familiar Shade' who will haunt Marlow, as Kurtz's own 'eloquent phantom' is destined to haunt him, for the rest of his days. Marlow sees them together in a moment that unites the woman's sorrow with her lover's death. He hears them together, the 'despairing regret' of her assertion of survival for ever mingling with 'the summing-up whisper of his eternal condemnation'.

The parallels go further still. At a crucial point in the conversation, the Intended 'put[s] out her arms as if after a retreating figure, stretching them black and with clasped pale hands across the fading and narrow sheen of the window' (page 120), and in so doing immediately reminds Marlow of the native woman – 'tragic also ... stretching bare brown arms over the glitter of the infernal stream' – who attended the departure of the steamboat from the Inner Station. Both women seek in their different ways to detain a departing god – the Intended by setting up the image of a mythic memory and offering to it the sacrifice of truth, her black counterpart by conjuring the physical continuation of an object of worship, a presence that is at best contradictory (an 'eloquent phantom') and at worst a hollow sham. Neither sees, nor apparently wishes to see, beyond the illusion, the particular lie that Kurtz embodies for her. Both, again, make their abode at the heart of one kind of darkness or another, and both have an intimacy with death.

From the very outset of his meeting with the Intended, Marlow realizes that 'surrendering' all that remains of Kurtz from his memory will be a considerably more difficult operation than he originally anticipated. As he enters the house, it seems that he carries with him a composite vision of the man as he lived: 'the stretcher, the phantom-bearers, the wild crowd of obedient worshippers, the gloom of the forests, the glitter of the reach between the murky bends, the beat of the drum, regular and muffled like the beating of a heart – the heart of a conquering darkness.' He sees it as a moment of victory for the wilderness – 'an invading and vengeful rush which, it seemed to me, I would have to keep back alone for the salvation of another soul' (page 116). All about him, however, he hears the dying man's whispered cry of 'The horror! The horror!' and, once inside the drawing-room, as we have already remarked, he senses the presence of Kurtz beside, if not actually commingled with, that of his fiancée. At once, 'with a sensation of panic in [his] heart', Marlow realizes that his visit is an enormous mistake, that he has 'blundered into a place of cruel and absurd mysteries not fit for a human being to behold'. It is, however, too late to retreat. Accordingly, throughout the interview, when he is not seeking refuge in discreet silence, he finds himself obliged to weigh his words carefully, to couch the agreement required of him in the most noncommittal of terms, and positively to suppress his tendency towards outrage, despair or 'dull anger'. For all his care in negotiating this conversational minefield, however, he is unable to avoid the trap he fears above all others, that of being forced to tell a lie.

30. The Lie (*page 121*)

Lying, as he made clear to his audience earlier in the story, is something that Marlow positively hates, for which he feels a near-physical aversion. To him, it has 'a taint of death, a flavour of mortality'.[1] Now, having admitted to the Intended that he was with Kurtz at the end and that he heard the dying man's 'very last words', he breaks off 'in a fright' at the realization that he cannot possibly say what those words were. More than ever he is aware of his powerlessness in the face of a triumphant darkness. He finds it impossible to believe, when the woman begs him to repeat Kurtz's deathbed utterance, that she cannot hear that ambiguous but 'persistent whisper' for herself. However, he pulls himself together and – out of the profound gloom that surrounds them – speaks slowly and deliberately the famous lie that it was her name.

Despite his earlier avowal of a profound personal aversion to lying, Marlow has – as Ian Watt reminds us[2] – already admitted to sacrificing truth to expediency on three previous occasions. These were when he led the brickmaker to believe that non-cooperation in the matter of securing the rivets necessary for repair of the steamer might lead to a setback in his career, his suppression (at the behest of the harlequin) of facts about Kurtz's life and beliefs both while still in Africa and since returning to Europe, and when – in order to prevent his participating in the native rituals – he assured Kurtz of his certain achievement of success in Europe. On each of these occasions, the truth was withheld or distorted for what, at the time, seemed a good reason. The same holds true here, in that the lie answers the pressing emotional need of the Intended to have 'something . . . to live for' and incidentally enables her to remain in what Marlow earlier described as 'that beautiful world of their own' in which women should be encouraged to avoid embroilment in the vicious and sordid affairs of men. The truth – the rendering to Kurtz of the 'justice' which is his due – might, under these particular circumstances, prove fatal to the Intended (at least in a figurative sense), being 'too dark altogether' for her to bear. The lie would at least offer some kind of hope or purpose for her life, however illusory Marlow might himself reckon such hope or purpose to be. But then, Marlow is – as his narrative has time and again conceded – scarcely the most reliable judge of the distinction between illusion and reality.

Marlow's acknowledgement of the complex and ambiguous rela-

100

tionship of truth and falsehood is reinforced by the commentary he makes on his feelings after speaking the lie. He fears that some appropriately fatal catastrophe will overtake him:

It seemed to me that the house would collapse before I could escape, that the heavens would fall upon my head. (page 121)

Nothing, however, happens. Perhaps the lie was not sufficiently momentous (when is a lie not a lie?). Perhaps the heavens might have fallen had he instead spoken the literal truth (what if the truth has the force of a lie, a lie the force of truth?). On this note of uncertainty, Marlow falls silent. Perhaps like Bacon's 'jesting Pilate', he senses that to such questions there are ultimately no satisfactory answers.

31. Conclusion (*page 121*)

At the beginning of Marlow's tale, the primary narrator warned that we were going to hear about one of his friend's 'inconclusive experiences'. As the story draws to its end, we might well feel inclined to concur with this judgement: for all its parallelism and structural integrity and for all its thematic insistence (light versus dark, the honesty of work versus the deceitfulness of words, restraint versus unfettered self-indulgence, moral and spiritual hollowness, the untrustworthiness of appearances and the ultimate nature of truth) *Heart of Darkness* is a narrative which works by means of suggestion rather than statement, is concerned with asking questions rather than providing pat answers.

That his audience has nevertheless been following Marlow's story with some interest is suggested by the revelation that they have failed to take full advantage of the turn of the tide. Marlow's figure, sitting as ever 'in the pose of a meditating Buddha', appears indistinct in the gloom – an apt reminder that his narrative is essentially reflective, that it is less concerned with the telling of what (by his own admission) is a fairly unremarkable story or the placing of a clear moral argument, than with a conscious process of spiritual cleansing enacted through a sort of 'introspective ordeal'.[1] It is a process which would not have been possible without the favourable coincidence of circumstance, setting and audience. That some kind of moral point is taken by at least one of the listeners aboard the *Nellie* is, however, suggested by the narrator's final observation that the brooding gloom which, at the beginning of the story, appeared to hover exclusively over – and indeed to be a physical embodiment of the evils perpetrated in – the city, has now spread across the entire sky: 'the tranquil waterway leading to the uttermost ends of the earth . . . seemed to lead into the heart of an immense darkness.'

Postscript

32. Konrad Korzeniowski and Joseph Conrad

Edward Garnett, author of one of the earliest reviews of *Heart of Darkness*, suggests that the piece is quintessentially an 'analysis of the deterioration of the white man's *morale*, when he is let loose from European restraint, and planted down in the tropics as an emissary of light armed to the teeth, to make trade profits out of the subject races'.[1] Conrad's response to this rather cut-and-dried reading was couched in appropriately ambiguous terms: 'My dearest fellow,' he wrote to Garnett, 'you quite overcome me. And your brave attempt to grapple with the fogginess of *Heart of Darkness*, to explain what I myself tried to shape blindfold, as it were, touched me profoundly.'[2] First serialized in *Blackwood's Magazine* during 1899, the novella had been virtually ignored by the critics for three years. It was not until its first hardback appearance in 1902 (together with *Youth* and *The End of the Tether*) that it began to arouse serious comment, though – even then – it was generally reckoned to be less accessible than its companion-pieces, 'too strong meat' (in Garnett's words) for 'the ordinary reader'. For all the unfamiliarity of Conrad's theme, however, and the problems which his narrative may have posed for the average reader, it is relevant to note that *Heart of Darkness* is closely tied to experiences which the author himself underwent some nine years prior to its publication. It is, furthermore, far from unique in this respect, since many of the fictitious adventures recounted in his writings have their roots in one phase or another of Conrad's action-packed career.

Joseph Conrad, the celebrated British author whose funeral took place at St Thomas's Roman Catholic Church in Canterbury on 7 August 1924, was born near Berdichev, in the Ukraine, on 3 December 1857, and christened Teodor Józef Konrad Nałęcz Korzeniowski. Both his parents came from well-to-do Polish families, his father, Apollo, being both an intellectual (he translated works by Victor Hugo and Alfred de Vigny from the French, and by Shakespeare from the English) and a political activist, dedicated to the achievement of an independent and unified Polish state.[3] He was frequently in trouble with the Russian authorities for organizing secret committees, leading angry public demonstrations and publishing highly inflammatory articles. Eventually, in the autumn of 1861, he was arrested, tried by a military tribunal and sent – together with his wife, Evelina, and their four-year-old son – into internal exile in a particularly inhospitable area of northern Russia. In the ensuing years, all three members of the family suffered from repeated bouts of ill health and depression. Eventually, in 1865, Evelina died of tuberculosis, to be followed, within three years, by her husband. By the age of twelve, Konrad Korzeniowski was an orphan.

From this point on, responsibility for the boy's upbringing was assumed by his maternal uncle, Tadeusz Bobrowski. It was this firm but kindly widower who made arrangements for Konrad's formal education and who responded to his nephew's restlessness and obvious distaste for school life by sending him, in May 1873, on an extended trip to Switzerland. About this time, Konrad seems to have developed a passion for the sea and repeatedly badgered his guardian to be allowed to join the French merchant navy. For a while, Bobrowski refused even to consider such an idea, but eventually adolescent persistence won the day. In mid-October 1874, Konrad set off by train for Marseilles. He was not yet seventeen, but was, to all intents and purposes, alone in the world.

The next four years saw Konrad Korzeniowski involved in a succession of colourful escapades – falling violently in and out of love, gun-running for Spanish Carlist insurgents, voyaging to the West Indies and Venezuela, making and losing large sums of money, and at one point (in 1878) apparently attempting suicide. The final drama – and the real turning point in his turbulent young life – came when the immigration authorities withdrew the permit that had, up till then, enabled him to serve in the French merchant fleet. Determined not to be thwarted in his maritime ambitions by what he saw as petty-minded bureaucracy, Korzeniowski sought employment elsewhere and was eventually taken on as an ordinary seaman aboard the British freighter *Mavis*. Thus began an association with British ships that was to last until he retired from the sea in 1894.

Service with the British merchant marine gave Korzeniowski the opportunity for further exotic travel, to ports around the Mediterranean, to Australia and (especially) to the East Indies. It also provided him with a respectable career and the prospect of promotion, and it led, in 1887, to his assumption of British citizenship. Above all, prolonged exposure to the society of British sailors and ex-patriate British communities around the world forced him to master the English language. So complete was his mastery, moreover, that when (in 1889) he made a serious start on his literary career,[4] he was able to do so not in Polish or French, the languages of his birth and upbringing, but in his adopted English. The transformation from K. N. Korzeniowski to Joseph Conrad was already well under way.

Konrad Korzeniowski and Joseph Conrad

The one significant interlude in Conrad's career as a British seaman came in 1890 when, unable to find a suitable merchant command, he signed on with the Brussels-based Société Anonyme Belge pour le Commerce du Haut-Congo as captain of one of that company's small steamers, used to ply the Congo River between Kinshasa and Stanley Falls. The painful experiences he underwent during his brief employment by the Société Anonyme were later to be transformed, at least in part, into those recounted by Marlow in *Heart of Darkness*.

33. Leopold II and the Congo

The territory to which Conrad travelled in 1890 (present-day Zaire) was known officially as the 'Congo Free State' and had, as such, been in existence for only five years. First visited by Portuguese explorers, it remained for decades largely uncharted and wholly undeveloped. The missionary activities of David Livingstone in the mid-1850s, together with the carefully publicized travels of Henry Morton Stanley some fifteen years later, did much to focus the attention of the European powers – especially those that were at the time looking to expand and consolidate their overseas colonies – on the existence and potential of the region.

The imperialist movement, of which this notorious 'scramble for Africa' was part, had its roots in Darwinian theory. Charles Darwin's treatise *On the Origin of Species* (first published in 1859) had aroused a good deal of public debate on account of its suggestion that, rather than being the products of a deliberate act of creation on the part of God, animal and plant species are the results of a process of natural selection. Evolutionary philosophers like Herbert Spencer, who had for some years been arguing that societies evolve in a similar way, were quick to seize on Darwin's theory of 'the preservation of favoured races in the struggle for life' as further support for their contention that 'the survival of the fittest' is a principle which operates throughout the universe. Theirs was a philosophy which could explain the existence of social inequality, with all its attendant evils, as a temporary but unavoidable stage on the evolutionary journey. It was a philosophy, moreover, which could readily be applied in the realm of international politics. In his brief but informative discussion of the Darwinian background to *Heart of Darkness*, Ian Watt points out that 'merely by occupying or controlling most of the globe, the European nations had demonstrated that they were the fittest to survive; and the exportation of their various economic, political and religious institutions was therefore a necessary step towards a higher form of human organization in the rest of the world.'[1] He goes on to note that Spencer became a prominent advocate of the notion that their inherited superiority had brought about the dominance of the white races, and that Darwin himself (in *The Descent of Man*, 1871) was soon categorizing races as 'high' or 'low', nations as 'stronger' or 'weaker'. That Marlow is himself receptive to Darwinian ideas is clear from his repeated use of the effective, if clichéd, metaphor of the darkness towards which he is constantly travelling. His voyage to the Inner Station becomes a species of counter-evolutionary time-travel:

Going up that river was like travelling back to the earliest beginnings of the world, when vegetation rioted on the earth and the big trees were kings ... We were wanderers on prehistoric earth, on an earth that wore the aspect of an unknown planet ... we were travelling in the night of first ages, of those ages that are gone, leaving hardly a sign – and no memories. (pages 66–9)

Such, then, was the philosophical climate which produced the Congo Free State. King Leopold II of the Belgians had been interested in the region for some time. He saw it as a means both of securing his personal fortune and establishing abroad the prestige of his tiny nation,[2] while at the same time proclaiming an altruistic desire 'to open to civilization the only part of our globe where Christianity has not yet penetrated and to pierce the darkness which envelops the entire population'.[3] Accordingly, in 1876, he promoted the foundation of the International Association for the Suppression of Slavery and the Opening Up of Central Africa, and secured the cooperation of Stanley in establishing a string of outposts along the Congo River. His ambitions were given a considerable fillip in 1884 when – at an international conference held in Berlin – he was granted personal ownership of and sole rule over the newly constituted Free State. In return, he was required to make several promises: one, that all nations would be accorded the right to trade freely within the territory's extensive boundaries; two, that he would not impose any kind of taxation on such trade; and three, that no nation (Belgium included) would be granted a monopoly on any item of trade. That Leopold signally failed to keep these promises, and that his regime was responsible for a whole catalogue of horrors, countenanced – if not carried out – in the name of civilization, are matters of history. As Hennessy remarks,[4] no sooner had he received the *fiat* of his European neighbours, than Leopold set about granting concessions to various companies and establishing the vast labour-pool without which they would find it impossible to operate. In this latter undertaking, his methods were, quite simply, machiavellian: with the cooperation of the native chiefs, he set up a system whereby work had the function of a tax medium, each individual being required to settle his liability by working for a specified period of time in return for minimum payment. It was, of course, slavery in everything but name: the so-called taxpayers were treated like prisoners and their work was carried out under the supervision of armed sentries.

Not surprisingly, the system lent itself 'to all kinds of tyranny, brutality and subsequent reprisals by the natives'.

A month and a half before Conrad's own arrival there, the black American lawyer and clergyman, George Washington Williams (who had been sent to study conditions in the Congo by the railway developer, Collis P. Huntington) wrote an open letter to Leopold from the settlement at Stanley Falls.[5] In it, he listed specific instances of corruption, mismanagement and atrocity practised by the Congo government, concluding his complaints with the following resounding plea:

Against the deceit, fraud, robberies, arson, murder, slave-raiding, and general policy of cruelty of your Majesty's Government to the natives, stands their [the natives'] record of unexampled patience, long-suffering and forgiving spirit, which put the boasted civilization and professed religion of your Majesty's Government to the blush . . .

All the crimes perpetuated in the Congo have been done in *your* name, and *you* must answer at the bar of Public Sentiment for the misgovernment of a people, whose lives were entrusted to you by the august Conference of Berlin, 1884–1885. I now appeal to the Powers who committed this infant State to your Majesty's charge, and to the great States which gave it international being; and whose majestic law you have scorned and trampled upon, to call and create an International Commission to investigate the charges herein preferred in the name of Humanity, Commerce, Constitutional Government and Christian Civilization . . .

I appeal to Anti-Slavery Societies in all parts of Christendom, to Philanthropists, Christians, Statesmen, and to the great mass of people everywhere, to call upon the Governments of Europe, to hasten the close of the tragedy your Majesty's unlimited Monarchy is enacting in the Congo.

Such outcries as Williams's, however, made little impact in Europe, where there was a general lack of interest in conditions prevailing in so distant and unfamiliar a part of the world, as well as a lack of sympathy for the outlook and lot of its native inhabitants. Under the circumstances, it was not difficult for Leopold to explain away the state of affairs for which he was responsible:

Wars do not necessarily mean the ruin of the regions in which they rage; our agents do not ignore this fact, so from the day when their effective superiority is affirmed, they feel profoundly reluctant to use force. The wretched negroes, however, who are still under the sole sway of their traditions, have that horrible belief that victory is only decisive when the enemy, fallen beneath their blows, is annihilated. The soldiers of the State, who are recruited necessarily from among the natives, do not immediately forsake those sanguinary habits that have been transmitted from generation to generation . . . I am pleased to think that our agents, nearly all of whom are volunteers drawn from the ranks of the Belgian army, have always present in their minds a strong sense of the career of honour in which they are engaged, and are animated with a pure feeling of patriotism; not sparing their own blood, they will the more spare the blood of the natives, who will see in them the all-powerful protectors of their lives and their property, benevolent teachers of whom they have so great a need.[6]

Conrad himself reflects on Leopold's cynical pursuit of his colonial goals under the guise of conducting 'a Crusade worthy of this century of progress' in a passage which he later deleted from the manuscript of *Heart of Darkness*. After noting the barefaced rapacity of Roman colonialism, that its practitioners 'grabbed what they could get for the sake of what was to be got', Marlow goes on:

That's all. The best of them is they didn't get up pretty fictions about it. Was there, I wonder, an association on a philanthropic basis to develop Britain, with some third-rate king for a president and solemn old senators discoursing about it approvingly and philosophers with uncombed beards praising it, and men in market places crying it up. Not much! And that's what I like![7]

34. Conrad's Congo Journey

The circumstances of Conrad's Congo journey are well documented in his own autobiographical writings, essays and journals which also put parts of Marlow's narrative in *Heart of Darkness* into interesting perspective. In 'Geography and Some Explorers',[1] for example, the author records his childhood fascination with the adventures of polar explorers like Franklin and McClintock, commenting on the purity of their scientific aims – they were, for him, untainted by the 'acquisitive spirit' of earlier navigators, whose motivation had been 'the idea of lucre in some form, the desire of trade or the desire of loot, disguised in more or less fine words' – as well as the romance of their endeavours. He credits Sir Leopold McClintock's account of *The Voyage of the 'Fox' in Arctic Seas* (which he probably first encountered in a French translation) with setting him off on 'romantic explorations of [his] inner self' and cultivating in him 'the taste of poring over maps':

Map-gazing, to which I became addicted so early, brings the problems of the great spaces of the earth into stimulating and directing contact with sane curiosity and gives an honest precision to one's imaginative faculty.

In due course, his interest shifted from Arctic geography to that of Africa, 'the continent out of which the Romans used to say some new thing was always coming':

Regions unknown! My imagination could depict to itself there worthy, adventurous and devoted men, nibbling at the edges, attacking from north and south and east and west, conquering a bit of truth here and bit of truth there, and sometimes swallowed up by the mystery their hearts were so persistently set on unveiling.

Elsewhere in his memoirs[2] Conrad recalls that – at about the age of nine – while he was one day poring over a map of Africa, he put his finger 'on the blank space then representing the unsolved mystery of that continent' and vowed 'with absolute assurance and an amazing audacity' to 'go *there*' (his italics) when he grew up. The '*there*' in question, he goes on to disclose, was 'the region of Stanley Falls . . . the blankest of blank spaces on the earth's figured surface'.

Thus when, in 1890, the occasion presented itself for Conrad to sail up the Congo River as far as Stanley Falls, he may well have seen in it an opportunity both to fulfil a long-cherished ambition and also to discover something about his own personality and motivation. As Ross C. Murfin observes, if mere stories of men like Franklin and McClintock were capable of stimulating the young Conrad's explorations of his inner self, 'how much more he was likely to learn about his own nature and human nature in general by travelling into the great expanse of white that lay beyond the coloured, mapped areas of Africa'.[3]

However, Conrad might never have seized the occasion had he not at the same time been beset with more material needs. To begin with, he was short of money. Moreover, although he had already, in 1886, passed the examinations which qualified him for command in the British merchant fleet, he had not – except for a brief spell on an Australian ship – been able to secure a captaincy. Accordingly, when – among other things – the distant prospect of commanding one of the Congo steamers owned by the Société Anonyme presented itself, he pursued it eagerly. In 1889, he travelled to Brussels to meet Captain Albert Thys, the company's managing director and a close associate of King Leopold. Their interview, however, was inconclusive, since there was no command currently available, and Conrad turned his attention instead to family matters. In April 1890 he was brought back to Brussels by the news that Thys (very likely substantially influenced in his decision by Conrad's cousin, Marguerite Poradowska, who happened to live in the Belgian capital) was prepared to offer him command of one of the company's steamers, the *Florida*. The position, he learned, had become vacant on account of the murder by natives of the previous captain, a man named Freisleben. Undeterred by this gloomy portent, he signed the necessary papers, made hasty preparations and took the train to Bordeaux whence he was to sail for Africa in the *Ville de Maceio*. Shortly before his departure, he wrote to a Polish relative that he was expecting to remain in the Congo for three years.

Conrad disembarked at Boma, at the mouth of the Congo River, where he joined a smaller vessel for the forty-mile journey upstream to Matadi, arriving there on 13 June 1890. At Matadi, he encountered a young Anglo-Irish agent, Roger Casement,[4] who was engaged in the construction of a railway link between that settlement and the one upriver at Kinshasa, thus by-passing some two hundred miles of intermittently unnavigable water. Casement, with whom he shared a room for a couple of weeks, was one of the few people Conrad encountered during his months in the Free State for whom he expressed any admiration or liking. Kinshasa was, in fact, Conrad's next destination, but, in the absence of rail or water transport he was obliged to make the journey there on foot. He was accompanied on this occasion by a party of thirty-one native bearers and another of the company's agents called Prosper Harou, who had travelled out with him on the *Ville de Maceio*. Within forty-eight hours of their departure, Harou seems to have fallen ill; he stayed ill, moreover, for the remainder of the journey, obliging the bearers to take turns in carrying him in a hammock and thus prompting frequent rows. Conrad's diary for this period[5] contains, along with brief descriptions of the terrain through which his party was travelling, some more ominous observations:

Thursday, 3rd July. Met an off[icer] of the State inspecting; a few minutes afterwards saw at a camp[in]g place the dead body of a Backongo. Shot? Horrid smell . . .

Friday, 4th July. Saw another dead body lying by the path in an attitude of meditative repose . . . At night when the moon rose heard shouts and drumming in distant villages. Passed a bad night . . .

Tuesday, 29th. Bad news from up the river. All the steamers disabled. One wrecked . . . On the road today passed a skeleton tied up to a post. Also white man's grave – no name. Heap of stones in the form of a cross . . .

Wednesday, 30th. Expect lots of bother with carriers tomorrow. Had them all called and made a speech which they did not understand . . .

Friday, 1st of August 1890. Chief came with a youth 13 suffering from gunshot wound in the head. Bullet entered about an inch above the right eyebrow . . .

On his arrival at Kinshasa the following day, Conrad was greeted with the news that – although the *Florida* had been salvaged and was currently undergoing repairs – he was to be attached as a supernumerary officer aboard another steamer, the *Roi des Belges*. Despite the fact that the attachment was to be temporary and was designed to help the new arrival familiarize himself with river navigation, Conrad was angry at what he saw as a deliberate attempt to cheat him of his command. Such public remonstrations as he made, however, were to no avail. The very next day (3 August 1890), the *Roi des Belges*, under the command of Captain Ludwig Koch, set out on the long voyage upriver to the settlement at Stanley Falls. Its purpose was to pick up the company's agent there – a man named Georges Antoine Klein – who was critically ill, and bring him back to Kinshasa for treatment. The principal passenger on this occasion was one Camille Delcommune, the Kinshasa station-manager who had also just been appointed acting-director of the Société Anonyme in the Congo. He was a man for whom Conrad appears to have conceived an almost instant dislike. The round trip was made in what, by contemporary standards, was record time: even so, Georges Klein did not survive for more than a few days of the journey downstream. Ironically, Conrad found himself in command of the *Roi des Belges* for part of the voyage, when Captain Koch himself fell sick. This was not sufficient to appease his feelings of outrage at the company and its activities, however, and – despite the promise of a ship of his own the following year – he determined to cut short his contract. It was a dysentery-racked and deeply disillusioned Conrad who set sail for Europe from Boma on 4 December 1890.

Partially selgish
& of words command T &

35. Joseph Conrad and Charlie Marlow

Jocelyn Baines reminds us of Conrad's assertion that *Heart of Darkness* is 'experience pushed a little (and only very little) beyond the actual facts of the case'.[1] Nor is it difficult for the reader to identify specific correspondences between places, events and characters. The 'Company Station', 'Central Station' and 'Inner Station' are clearly the settlements at Matadi, Kinshasa and Stanley Falls, respectively. The circumstances of Marlow's visit to Africa and details of his upriver journey have a good deal in common with those described – albeit piecemeal – in Conrad's own letters, journals and memoirs. Moreover, many of the novella's characters, from Fresleven to the corpse of the 'middle-aged negro, with a bullet in the forehead' over which Marlow literally stumbles in the course of his overland journey, have recognizable historical counterparts. Part of Conrad's purpose in suppressing or changing real names is, of course, to endow his subject matter with greater universality while, at the same time, intensifying the sense of mystery that is so vital to the narrative. Such changes may also, however, be part of a process of conscious distancing of Marlow's fictitious experiences from the author's real ones. As Murfin points out,[2] no matter how tempting it may be for the reader to think of *Heart of Darkness* as thinly veiled autobiography, there are positive dangers in doing so. He cites the formalist view that 'a work of art ... is not undigested experience' but is 'characterized by *form*', and he notes that this form is to be discovered 'by finding the patterns and relationships that exist within the work itself, not the connections that may seem to exist between the work and its author's life story'. Accordingly, he is at pains to balance appreciation of the undoubted similarities that exist between Conrad's and Marlow's Congo experiences with a number of emphatic differences, and in this he is supported by several other recent commentators.[3]

To begin with, the Congo up which Conrad sailed in 1890 was in fact a better charted and a good deal busier waterway than that described by Marlow. The emptiness and silence on which the latter comments – his sense of being 'bewitched and cut off for ever from everything' he once knew – provide a useful reminder, however, that his journey is as much one of exploration as of rescue, and that it constitutes a fulfilment of his long-cherished ambition to travel to one of the last 'blank spaces' on the earth. Some of the events that take place in the course of his journey also depart significantly from those recorded in Conrad's journals. For example, whereas Marlow waits for some time at the Central Station while his crippled vessel is repaired and then takes command on her journey upriver to relieve Kurtz, Conrad – who had taken almost twice as long as he should have done to cover the two hundred miles from Matadi – was obliged to set out for Stanley Falls immediately upon his arrival in Kinshasa and did so, not as captain of the *Roi des Belges*, but as assistant to Captain Koch. The effect of this change is, of course, to place Marlow squarely at the centre of exciting and dangerous action, while Conrad himself was little more than an observer on a routine voyage.

The chief differences between text and life lie, as one might expect, in the area of characterization. While we may be able to detect something of the personality of Captain Thys in that of the 'pale plumpness' whom Marlow meets at the Company's European headquarters, while the flabby agent whose illness causes repeated and irritating delays in the journey to the Central Station is clearly based on Prosper Harou, and while the Manager of the Central Station shares with Camille Delcommune the Conradian opprobrium of being 'a common trader', certain other correspondences are notably lacking. We search the historical sources in vain, for instance, for figures on whom the brickmaker, the harlequin or Kurtz's Intended might have been modelled. Furthermore, even where it is possible to detect correspondences between fictional characters and real ones, it is almost certainly unwise to push them too far. Similarities between the Chief Accountant, for whose 'unexpected elegance of get-up' Marlow expresses a mild admiration, and Roger Casement are mostly superficial. More importantly, likenesses between Kurtz and Georges Antoine Klein appear to be limited to the problematical circumstances in which the two men find themselves. There is no evidence to suggest that Klein was in fact any more than an unremarkable company functionary, and it is now generally accepted that Conrad drew for the character of Kurtz on a number of contemporary figures to details of whose personalities and exploits he had access through his reading of the newspapers. And it is highly appropriate that this should be the case, since – as we have seen in the course of this commentary – at several points in *Heart of Darkness*, Conrad presents Kurtz as a foil or counterpart to Marlow, reminding the reader of the dangers that lie in wait for every man (even an 'emissary of light') who elects to confront the darkness. We should remember, too, that the story Marlow himself relates is far from being a simple record of exactly remembered events.

He refers repeatedly to the dream-like quality of his experiences and makes it clear that initial observations and interpretations of events are not to be trusted. Moreover, on at least one occasion (shortly after his account of the attack on the steamboat) he falls into a distracted silence, apparently losing the thread of his story in a maze of private thoughts and associations:

'Oh, yes, I heard more than enough. And I was right too. A voice. He was very little more than a voice. And I heard – him – it – this voice – other voices – all of them were so little more than voices – and the memory of that time itself lingers around me, impalpable, like a dying vibration of one immense jabber, silly, atrocious, sordid, savage, or simply mean, without any kind of sense. Voices, voices – even the girl herself – now –'

He was silent for a long time.

'I laid the ghost of his gifts at last with a lie,' he began, suddenly. 'Girl! What? Did I mention a girl? Oh, she is out of it – completely. They – the women I mean – are out of it – should be out of it.' (page 84)

Indeed, by the conclusion of Marlow's narrative, we cannot be sure that even he really knows what he has been telling his audience aboard the *Nellie*. And the problem is further compounded for us by the fact that the whole tale is presented as hearsay, filtered through the (presumably) selective consciousness of the unnamed primary narrator.

36. *Heart of Darkness in 1899*

Given his background – his Polish upbringing, his turbulent adolescence, his extensive seagoing career – it would not have been surprising had Joseph Conrad made his mark on the British literary scene as a colourful primitive, a teller of action-packed but ultimately insubstantial tales. However, even the most casual acquaintance with a work like *Heart of Darkness* – with its complex narrative structure and its treatment of major moral issues – is enough to persuade the reader of the high level of its author's literary and intellectual sophistication. Critics are, in fact, generally agreed in seeing Conrad as a member of the early twentieth-century modernist movement, a distinction he shares with such writers as Virginia Woolf, James Joyce and T. S. Eliot.

The modernists were – like all comparable artistic groupings – a distinctly heterogeneous body, as much noted for their differences as for what they had in common. Nevertheless, many of their writings bear witness to a shared interest both in technical experimentation and in current anthropological and psychological thinking. Their technical experimentation was concerned, in the main, with moving away from such traditional nineteenth-century devices as step-by-step exposition and objective realism, and embracing instead the narrative method now generally known as 'stream-of-consciousness'. This expression, first coined by the American philosopher William James in his *Principles of Psychology* (1890), graphically conveys the manner in which a character's unspoken thoughts, feelings and associations flow through his or her waking mind in a random, sometimes disorderly, fashion. On some occasions, interior monologue replaces conventional dialogue, while on others, the form and syntax of the dialogue are distorted by the arbitrary nature of the thought-processes from which it springs. *Heart of Darkness* contains some notable examples of the operation of this method, moments where the articulation of Marlow's private thoughts threatens the chronology and the coherence of his narrative. At the very opening of his tale, he is at pains to establish a clear storyline for the benefit of his listeners:

I don't want to bother you much with what happened to me personally ... yet to understand the effect of it on me you ought to know how I got out there, what I saw, how I went up that river to the place where I first met the poor chap. It was the farthest point of navigation [. . .]

Having done so, however, he immediately invites confusion by launching into a passage of extended subjective reflection:

[. . .] and the culminating point of my experience. It seemed somehow to throw a kind of light on everything about me – and into my thoughts. It was sombre enough, too – and pitiful – not extraordinary in any way – not very clear either. No, not very clear. And yet it seemed to throw a kind of light. (page 32)

Another, and perhaps even more telling, example of this same tendency is to be found in the passage, quoted above, that centres on the long break in Marlow's narrative and surprises listeners and reader alike with its first mention of 'the girl' in the story.

Two of the greatest contemporary influences on modernist writers are generally acknowledged to have been Sir James Frazer and Sigmund Freud. Frazer, an agnostic and arguably the leading social anthropologist of his day, is now best remembered for his comparative study of man's belief systems and institutions, *The Golden Bough*, the first of whose twelve volumes appeared in 1890, the very year that Conrad made his Congo journey. The principal focus of Frazer's work is on human progress – over time – from magical to religious and ultimately to scientific modes of thought. His discussion of the first of these stages contains examples of fertility cults, of the ritual of the scapegoat, of the deification of living kings and chieftains, and of the ritual sacrifice of such leaders to forestall their abandonment of the tribe or their death from natural causes: 'In the kingdom of Congo, there was a supreme pontiff . . . and if he were to die a natural death, they thought that the world would perish.'[1] It is clearly a short step from such discussions to Conrad's story, however he came by it, of a man who 'preside[d] at certain midnight dances ending with unspeakable rites', of whom the harlequin asserts that his tribe 'adored him' to the point of possessiveness, and whose imminent departure produces what for the Europeans aboard the steamboat is a wild and terrifying demonstration of tribal will:

There was an eddy in the mass of human bodies, and the woman with helmeted head and tawny cheeks rushed out to the very brink of the stream. She put out her hands, shouted something, and all that wild mob took up the shout in a roaring chorus of articulated, rapid, breathless utterance. (page 109)

There is an understandable hesitancy among modern commentators to see *Heart of Darkness* as being directly affected by Freudian psychoanalytic theory, since *Die Traumdeutung*, Freud's enormously influential study of the relationship between dreams, repression and the conscious state, was not published until 1900, the year after the novella's first appearance. Nevertheless, some interesting connections exist. The main thrust of *Die Traumdeutung* ('The Interpretation of Dreams') is to establish that dreams are manifestations of urges or desires (mainly sexual in origin) that have been repressed by the individual's *ego* or conscious mind. These urges, Freud contends, have their origin in the *id*, a huge storehouse of irrational mental activity, comprising – among other things – a whole range of sexual, emotional and aggressive impulses. The conscious mind rejects and represses such impulses because they are at odds with civilized conduct, but it is unable to destroy them. They live on in the *id* and are able to encroach on the consciousness when, in states of sleep or day-dreaming, the *ego*'s control is relaxed. It is the purpose of the psychoanalyst, by minutely examining an individual's dream sequences, to establish the identity and origin of his or her repressed impulses.

The most obvious connection between such theories and *Heart of Darkness* lies in Marlow's repeated assertion of the dream-quality surrounding many of his experiences. He begins, as we have seen, by explaining that nothing he observed in the course of his journey appeared 'very clear' to him. Later, after his account of his conversation with the brickmaker, he complains of the impossibility of his undertaking:

> Do you see the story? Do you see anything? It seems to me I am trying to tell you a dream – making a vain attempt, because no relation of a dream can convey . . . that commingling of absurdity, surprise, and bewilderment in a tremor of struggling revolt, that notion of being captured by the incredible which is of the very essence of dreams . . . (page 57)

As his little vessel makes its way upstream, he is constantly struck by the unearthliness of his surroundings and by the almost totally incomprehensible otherness of the native inhabitants. For days on end, his life is pervaded by dream-sensations, a fact which contributes – on a number of significant occasions – to his mistaking appearance for reality. With his arrival at the Inner Station, his dream assumes more sinister proportions and Kurtz, once an object of his admiring interest, becomes 'the nightmare of [his] choice'.

Even though the dream we have been following is Marlow's, it is in Kurtz that we see what must inevitably happen when an individual is dominated by the all-consuming and unquenchable appetite of the *id*. On the other hand, Conrad has been at pains throughout the novella to emphasize the common background and outlook of the two men, to

121

suggest that what happens to the one could equally happen to the other. We recall how the 'wild and passionate uproar' of their dancing arouses in Marlow a sense of remote kinship with the natives –

if you were man enough you would admit to yourself that there was in you just the faintest trace of a response to the terrible frankness of that noise, a dim suspicion of there being a meaning in it which you – you so remote from the night of first ages – could comprehend. (page 69)

– and we understand that the temptation to atavistic reversion is universal.

In this way, Conrad's own journey up the Congo River in 1890 has been transformed, first, into a fiction about a man's venture into the physically unknown, and second, into an account of a 'psychological journey into the darkness of the human unconscious'.[2] In satisfying his childhood longing for self-discovery, for 'explorations of [his] inner self', Conrad has provided a means by which we, his readers, may better understand our own nature.

Notes

1 Introduction

1 Ian Watt, *Conrad in the Nineteenth Century* (Berkeley and Los Angeles: University of California Press, 1979), pp. 199–200.

2 The *Nellie* and Her Crew

1 William Bysshe Stein, 'The Lotus Posture and the *Heart of Darkness*', *Modern Fiction Studies*, II, 4 (Winter 1956–7), pp. 235–7.

2 Seymour Gross, 'A Further Note on the Function of the Frame in *Heart of Darkness*', *Modern Fiction Studies*, III, 2 (Summer 1957), pp. 167–70.

3 The Setting

1 Robert O. Evans, 'Conrad's Underworld', *Modern Fiction Studies*, II (May 1956), pp. 56–62.

4 Marlow's Preamble

1 Watt, *Conrad in the Nineteenth Century*, p. 216.

7 The Company Headquarters

1 Lillian Feder, 'Marlow's Descent into Hell', *Nineteenth Century Fiction*, IX (1955), pp. 280–92; Evans, 'Conrad's Underworld'.

2 Watt, *Conrad in the Nineteenth Century*, pp. 189–96.

3 Robert S. Baker, in his review of Ian Watt's *Conrad in the Nineteenth Century* (*Contemporary Literature*, XXII, 1981, pp. 116–26), insists that these two black-clad receptionists represent Clotho and Lachesis, while the third Fate – their sister Atropos – makes her appearance later in the novella.

13 The General Manager

1 Richard Curle (ed.), *Conrad to a Friend: 150 Selected Letters from Joseph Conrad to Richard Curle* (London: Sampson Low, Marston, 1928), p. 142.

15 Marlow

1 Jerome Thale, 'Marlow's Quest', *University of Toronto Quarterly*, XXIV (July 1955), pp. 351–8.
2 Feder, 'Marlow's Descent into Hell'.

17 The River Journey

1 Chinua Achebe, 'An Image of Africa: Racism in Conrad's *Heart of Darkness*', *The Massachusetts Review*, 18 (1977), pp. 782–94.

19 Events in the Fog

1 Achebe, 'An Image of Africa: Racism in Conrad's *Heart of Darkness*'.

20 Marlow's Errors of Judgement

1 Ian Watt, in *Conrad in the Nineteenth Century*, pp. 169–80, provides a useful section on this topic, which is also taken up in Bruce Johnson, 'Conrad's Impressionism and Watt's "Delayed Decoding"', in Ross C. Murfin (ed.), *Conrad Revisited: Essays for the Eighties* (University of Alabama Press, 1985), pp. 51–70.

22 Marlow's Digression: the Character of Kurtz

1 Some suggestions as to why this should be the case are made in Stephen A. Reid, 'The "Unspeakable Rites" in *Heart of Darkness*', *Modern Fiction Studies*, IX, 4 (Winter 1963–4), pp. 347–56.

25 Enter Kurtz

1 See especially Baker's review of Ian Watt's *Conrad in the Nineteenth Century*.

26 Marlow's Mission Ashore

1 Watt, *Conrad in the Nineteenth Century*, pp. 231–2.

27 The Death of Kurtz

1 Cedric Watts, *A Preface to Conrad* (Harlow: Longman, 1982), pp. 129–31.

29 The Intended

1 Feder, 'Marlow's Descent into Hell'.

30 The Lie

1 Garrett Stewart, 'Lying as Dying in *Heart of Darkness*', *PMLA*, 95 (1980), pp. 319–31, contains some thoughtful observations on this subject.

2 Watt, *Conrad in the Nineteenth Century*, p. 242.

31 Conclusion

1 Stein, 'The Lotus Posture and the *Heart of Darkness*'.

32 Konrad Korzeniowski and Joseph Conrad

1 Edward Garnett, unsigned review in *Academy and Literature*, 6 December 1902, quoted in Norman Sherry (ed.), *Conrad: The Critical Heritage* (London: Routledge & Kegan Paul, 1973), pp. 132–3.

2 Laurence Davies and Frederick R. Karl (eds.), *The Collected Letters of Joseph Conrad* (Cambridge University Press, 1983), vol. 2, pp. 467–8.

3 Since the last quarter of the eighteenth century Poland had effectively ceased to exist, its territories having been carved up and shared between the Russian, Prussian and Austro-Hungarian empires.

4 Conrad actually submitted a short story entitled 'The Black Mate' for a competition in the magazine *Tit-Bits* as early as 1886. However, it was not accepted, and the original was apparently lost. Conrad's next literary undertaking seems to have been the composition of the novel *Almayer's Folly*, started in 1889. A revised version of 'The Black Mate' was, however, published in the *London Magazine* in 1902. A documented discussion of Conrad's first ventures into the world of writers is to be found in Jocelyn Baines, *Joseph Conrad: A Critical Biography* (London: Weidenfeld & Nicolson, 1960), pp. 84–5.

33 Leopold II and the Congo

1 Watt, *Conrad in the Nineteenth Century*, p. 156.

2 Leopold II had ruled since 1865. Compared with his father (Leopold I, elected first king of the Belgians in 1831), he was a generally unpopular monarch and used his Congo connections to bolster both his nation's commercial prowess and his personal reputation.

3 Quoted in Maurice N. Hennessy, *Congo: A Brief History and Appraisal* (London: Pall Mall Press, 1961), p. 13.

4 Ibid., pp. 13–27.

5 George Washington Williams, *An Open Letter to His Serene Majesty Leopold II, King of the Belgians and Sovereign of the Independent State of Congo*, reprinted in John Hope Franklin, *George Washington Williams: A Biography* (University of Chicago Press, 1985), pp. 243–54.

6 Quoted in Guy Burrows, *The Land of the Pigmies* (London, 1898), p. 286.

7 Joseph Conrad, *Heart of Darkness*, Norton Critical Edition, ed. Robert Kimbrough (New York: W. W. Norton, 1988), p. 10.

34 Conrad's Congo Journey

1 Published in Joseph Conrad, *Last Essays*, ed. Richard Curle (London: Dent, 1926).

2 Joseph Conrad, *A Personal Record* (London: Dent, 1912), p. 13.

3 Ross C. Murfin (ed.), *Heart of Darkness: A Case Study in Contemporary Criticism* (New York: St Martin's Press, 1989), p. 8.

4 An active opponent of slavery in the Congo Free State, Casement later became British consular official at Boma. Knighted in 1911, he was subsequently degraded and executed, having been found guilty of treasonable participation in the Sinn Fein rebellion.

5 Reproduced in Joseph Conrad, *Congo Diary and Other Uncollected Pieces*, ed. Zdzislaw Najder (New York: Doubleday, 1978).

35 Joseph Conrad and Charlie Marlow

1 Baines, *Joseph Conrad: A Critical Biography*, p. 117.

2 Murfin, *Heart of Darkness: A Case Study in Contemporary Criticism*, p. 13.

3 Notably Norman Sherry in his study *Conrad's Western World* (Cambridge

University Press, 1971), and Paul O'Prey in his introduction to the Penguin Twentieth-Century Classics edition of *Heart of Darkness* (Harmondsworth, 1989).

4 See Watt, *Conrad in the Nineteenth Century*, pp. 142–4.

36 *Heart of Darkness* in 1899

1 J. G. Frazer, *The Golden Bough*, 2 vols. (London: 1894), vol. 1, p. 113.

2 Brook Thomas, 'Preserving and Keeping Order by Killing Time in *Heart of Darkness*', reprinted in Murfin, *Heart of Darkness: A Case Study in Contemporary Criticism*, pp. 237–55.

Discover more about our forthcoming books through Penguin's FREE newspaper...

It's packed with:

- exciting features
- author interviews
- previews & reviews
- books from your favourite films & TV series
- exclusive competitions & much, much more...

Write off for your free copy today to:
Dept JC
Penguin Books Ltd
FREEPOST
West Drayton
Middlesex
UB7 0BR
NO STAMP REQUIRED

READ MORE IN PENGUIN

CRITICAL STUDIES

Described by *The Times Educational Supplement* as 'admirable' and 'superb', Penguin Critical Studies is a specially developed series of critical essays on the major works of literature for use by students in universities, colleges and schools.

Titles published or in preparation include:

William Blake
The Changeling
Doctor Faustus
Emma and Persuasion
Great Expectations
The Great Gatsby
Heart of Darkness
The Poetry of Gerard
  Manley Hopkins
Joseph Andrews
Mansfield Park
Middlemarch
The Mill on the Floss
Paradise Lost
The Poetry of Alexander
  Pope

The Portrait of a Lady
A Portrait of the Artist as a
  Young Man
The Return of the Native
Rosencrantz and Guildenstern
  are Dead
Sons and Lovers
Tennyson
Tess of the D'Urbervilles
To the Lighthouse
The Waste Land
Wordsworth
Wuthering Heights
Yeats

READ MORE IN PENGUIN

CRITICAL STUDIES

Described by *The Times Educational Supplement* as 'admirable' and 'superb', Penguin Critical Studies is a specially developed series of critical essays on the major works of literature for use by students in universities, colleges and schools.

Titles published or in preparation include: